Unearthing Science

by Sara Zimmerman

For information, please contact Sara Zimmerman at info@unearthedcomics.com
P.O. Box 4051, Truckee, CA 96160.

ISBN-13: 978-0615918464
ISBN-10: 0615918468

First edition 2013

www.UnearthedComics.com

Cover art: Sara Zimmerman

Dedication:

To Cali and all the curious minds of the world.

Acknowledgements:

Unearthed Comics is here because of the undying love and support of my husband, daughter, family, friends, and fans. Because of you and all of my loving Kickstarter supporters, *Unearthed Comics: Unearthing Science* has come to fruition. I am so grateful for all of you!

Thank you, Kickstarter backers (shown in no particular order):

Tom & Barbara Bray
Tim & Terry Leach
Sandy Ritz
Julianne Zimmerman
Kim & Carbys Zimmerman
Karen Bray
Michelle Turley
Nicole Janoschek
Ali Leach
Cathy Bray
Peter & Janice Bray
Phil Thomas
Karen Terrey
Ann Sheppard
Nick Seluk
Barbara & George Butko
Jon Rombach
Annie Nelson
Carrie L Little
Mel Dumenko
Teri Nouchi Haye
John Evans
Robert Williams
Shirley Clark

Adrian Beffa
William Steele
Julie Spradley
Franklin Rohan
Sandy Korth
Lizzie Ellis
Lara Kilpatrick
Lynn Sorrentino
Vanessa Porter
Jason Neal Morgan
John Neininger
Lowell Tyler
Lise Rode
Anne Norloff
Sonja & Dan Martin
Amy Momb
Ted Miles
Donna Saufley
Ryan Quint
Mimi Rondenet
Cristal Guzman
Bones
Kirsten Schneider
Mickaël Pesquet

John Prichard
Kamara D Climber
Lara Pearson
Julia Worster
Jessica Lee
Mark Glavin
Jami Wardman
Iliese Bowman
Lauren Schurmeier
Bob McCullough
Jesse Kiefer
Dunja Lavrova
Anne Marie Amyot
Eric Larson
Jeffrey Price
Catherine One III
Taryn Washburn
Lauren Stern
Aja Yee
Thomas Edlen
Karin & Aaron Abraham
Charles Pineo
Jan Miletich
Chandra Wade

Lisa Pearson
Maya Choucair Hamade
Tracie Mulvin
Tim Hauserman
Chris Grady
Bridget Horn
Lisa McGuiness
Mary Rae Gallegos
Eric Crowe
Eagle Archambeault
Sara Armstrong
Estelle Robichaux
Ami & Matt Vannoy
Lara Walker
Stephen McGee
Steve Klinetobe
Justin Voss
James L. Smith
Sue Whitaker
Mayumi Elegado
Robert J. Schimmel
Madeleine Holly-Rosing
Derena Ryan McCray
Dorene Kordal

Katie McKissick
Donald Harper
Kit Fraser
Aviva Rossi
Sara Dube
Dave Mercier
Amy Hakanson
Ann Whitney
Nicholas Harman
Joslyn Neiderer
Laurel Galm
Sara Conrad
Angela Eaton
Daphne Hougard
Dulce Gross
Esme Purdie
Robert Price
Kimberly Kaznowski
Ariel Weaver
David Zougui
Anibal Ramirez
John Coveyou
Jessica Hall
E. Smithe
Christian Green

And a big thank you to all of the people who have lovingly shared my comics on their sites and connected with me on Facebook, Twitter and Pinterest. I feel like I have a new, virtual family!

Author's note:

I've always loved the outdoors; from the first days that my parents let me eat dirt, my grandparents taught me how to garden, and my friends played with me beneath the stars. This incredible world continues to intrigue me as I grow; whether I am trying to identify which bird is flying over me during a hike, the composition of the boulder I'm climbing, or where to catch the perfect wave with a particular swell direction. Since the outdoors is Nature's gateway drug to science, I naturally became interested in how and why the world works in such a wonderful way.

Though I pursued a degree in Environmental Studies, I am by no means a formal scientist. I'm just an artist who gets excited about thoughts, the world, and curious minds. For this book, I decided to focus on science-related comics because I love the thought of people pushing themselves, diverting their focus from the inconsequential drab promoted through the media, and working towards new ideas and hopeful solutions to challenging problems. The purpose of Unearthed Comics: Unearthing Science is to take science one step further and to be able to find the humor in what are usually areas of intense focus (and often, very serious studies). However, if you see something scientifically incorrect, just take a step back and absorb the humor of the larger picture. After all, science is for curious and open minds (and you can't keep an open mind without a little humor).

Oh, and here's my public service announcement since I already have your attention:
Be sure to live and explore "science" consciously so you can do what you can to contribute to a better world.

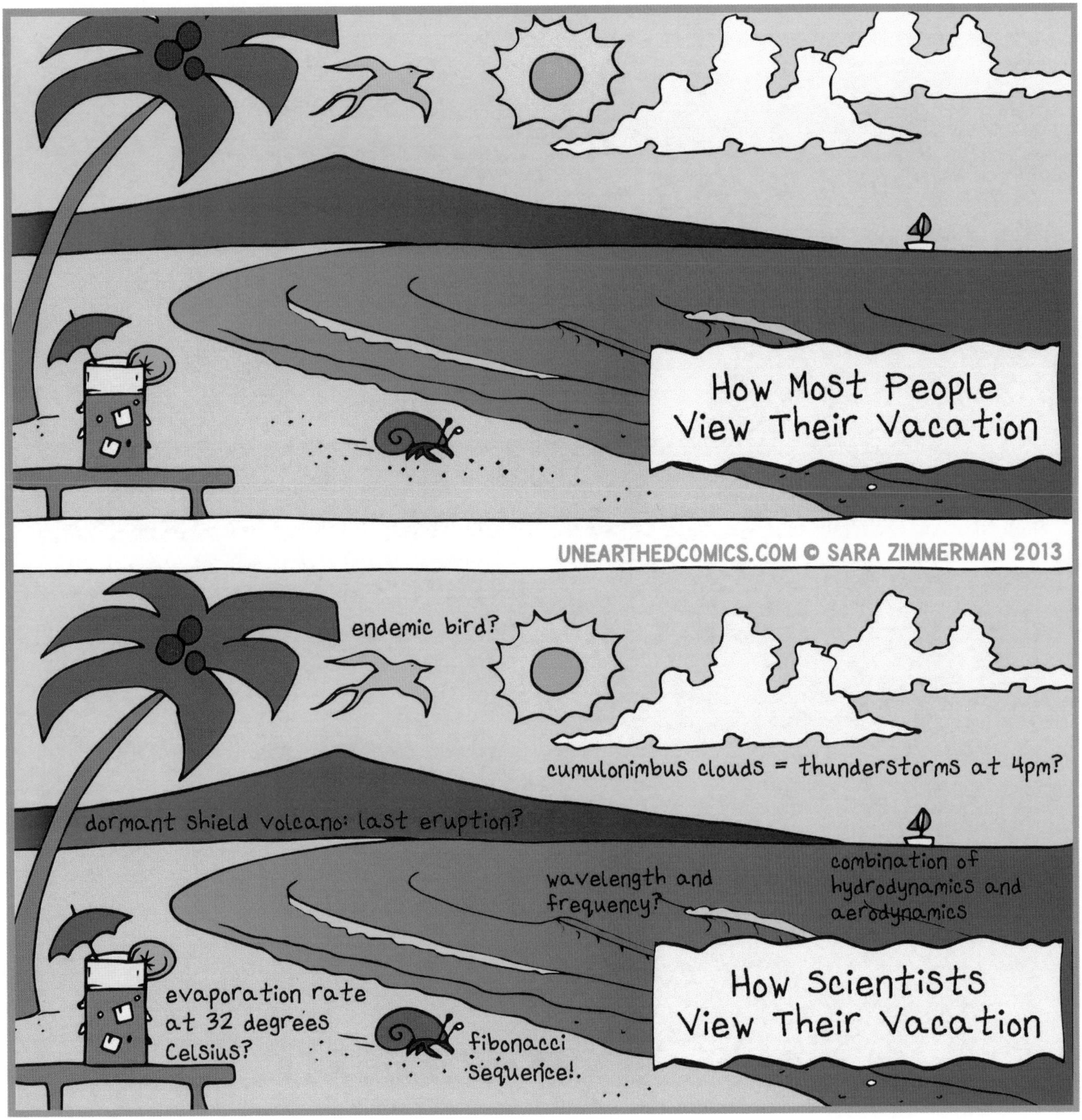
How Most People View Their Vacation
UNEARTHEDCOMICS.COM © SARA ZIMMERMAN 2013
endemic bird?
cumulonimbus clouds = thunderstorms at 4pm?
dormant shield volcano: last eruption?
wavelength and frequency?
combination of hydrodynamics and aerodynamics
evaporation rate at 32 degrees Celsius?
fibonacci sequence!
How Scientists View Their Vacation

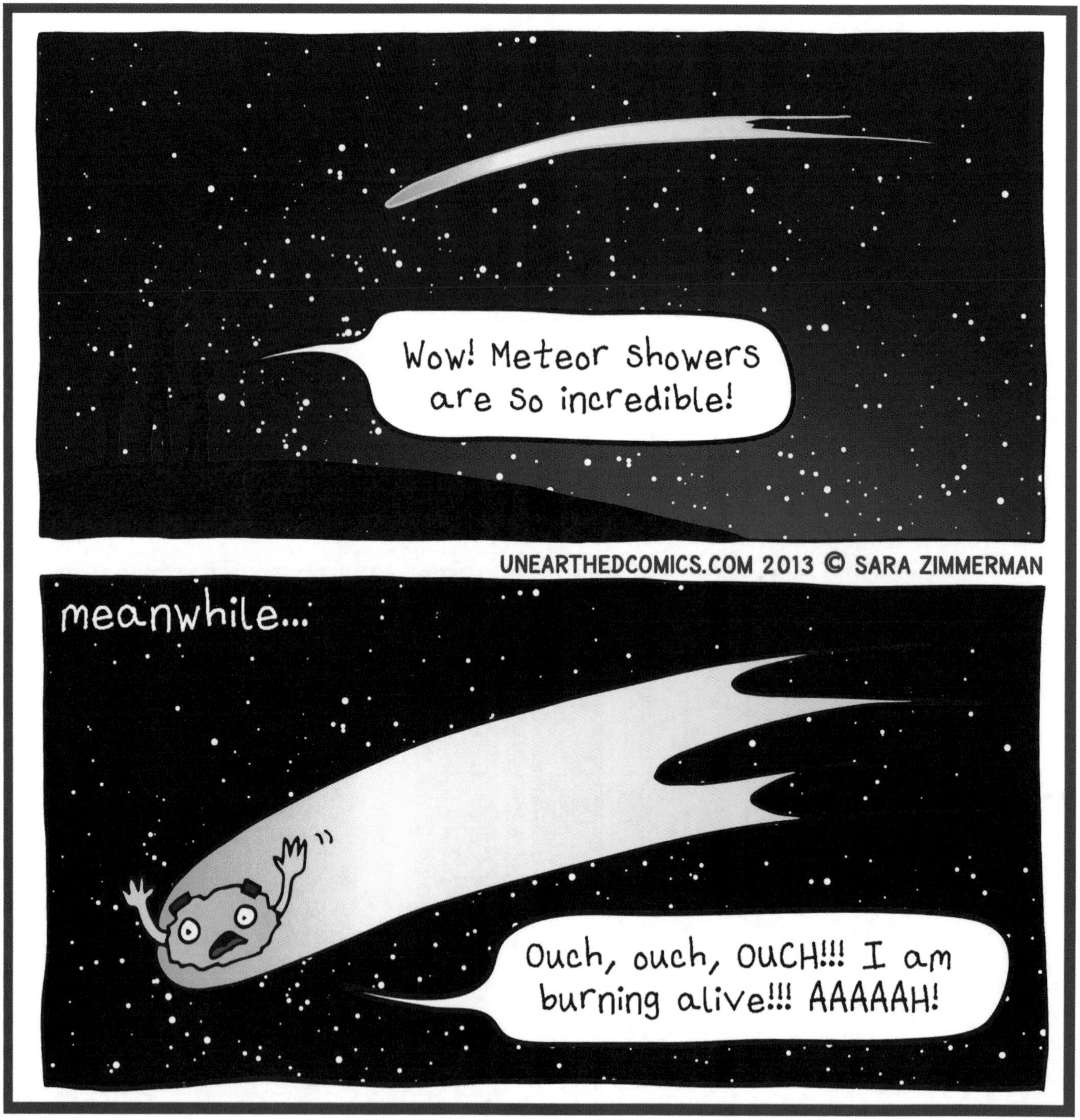
Wow! Meteor showers are so incredible!
UNEARTHEDCOMICS.COM 2013 © SARA ZIMMERMAN
meanwhile...
Ouch, ouch, OUCH!!! I am burning alive!!! AAAAAH!

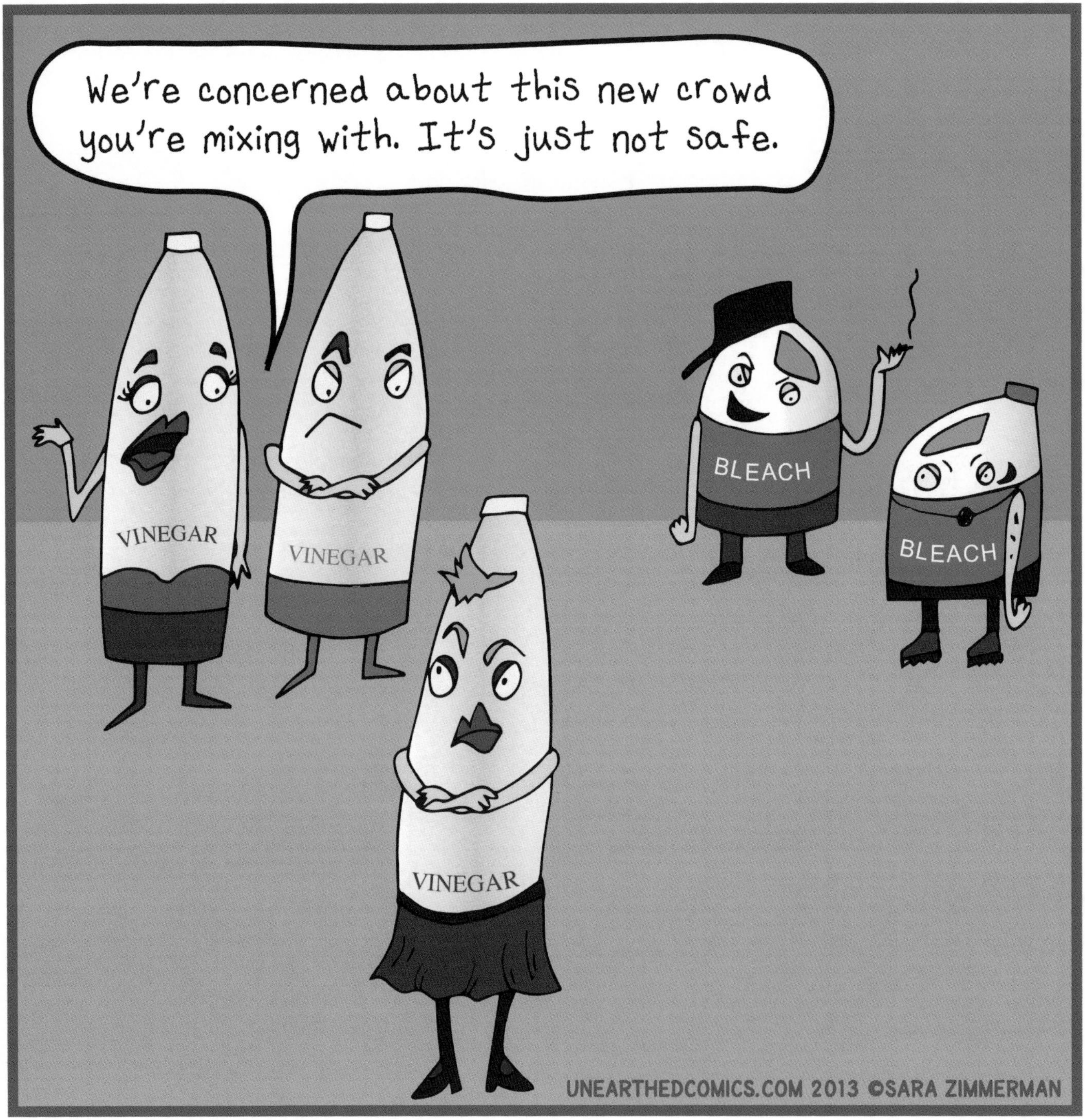
We're concerned about this new crowd you're mixing with. It's just not safe.
VINEGAR
VINEGAR
BLEACH
BLEACH
VINEGAR
UNEARTHEDCOMICS.COM 2013 ©SARA ZIMMERMAN

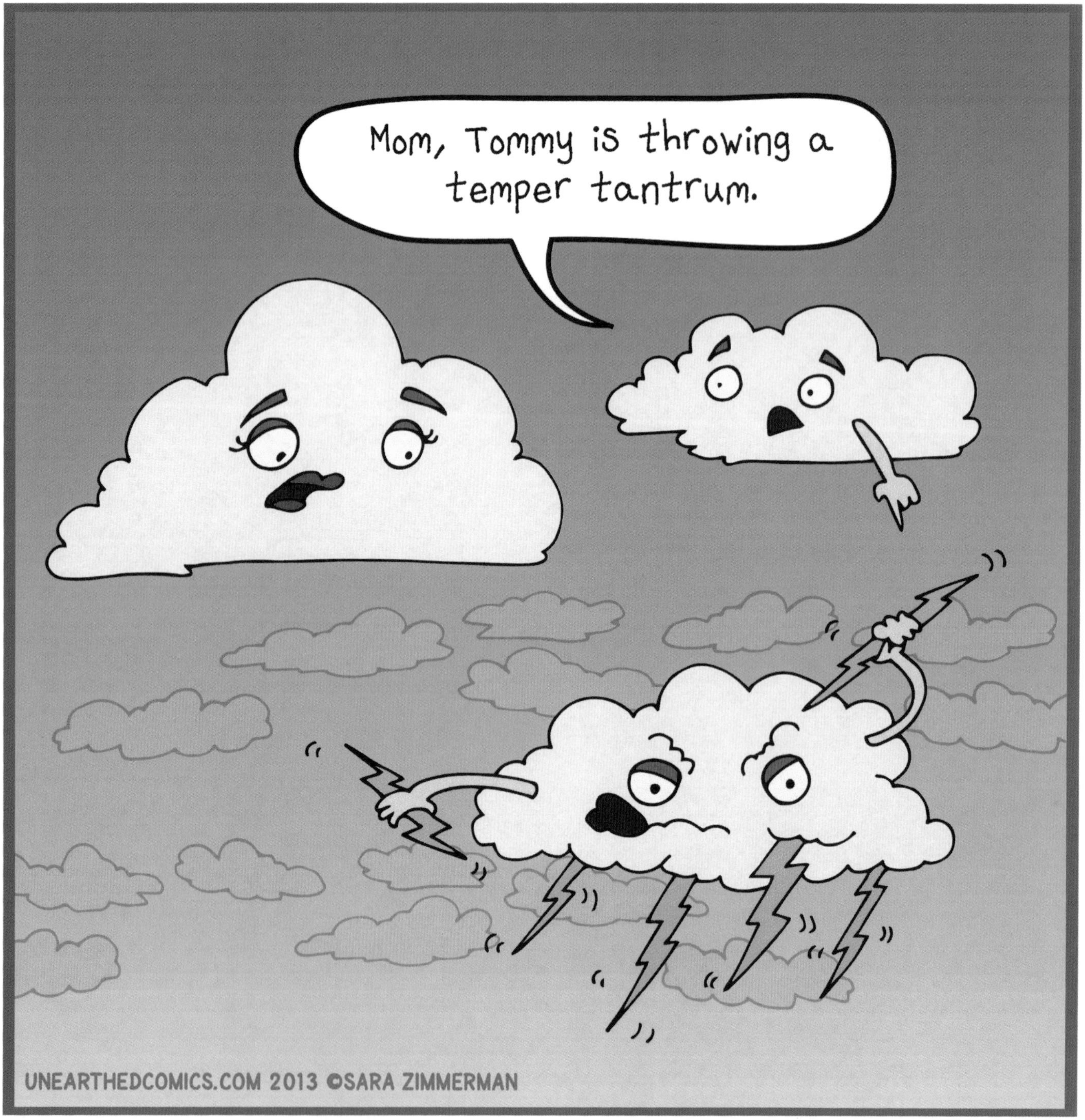
Mom, Tommy is throwing a temper tantrum.
UNEARTHEDCOMICS.COM 2013 ©SARA ZIMMERMAN

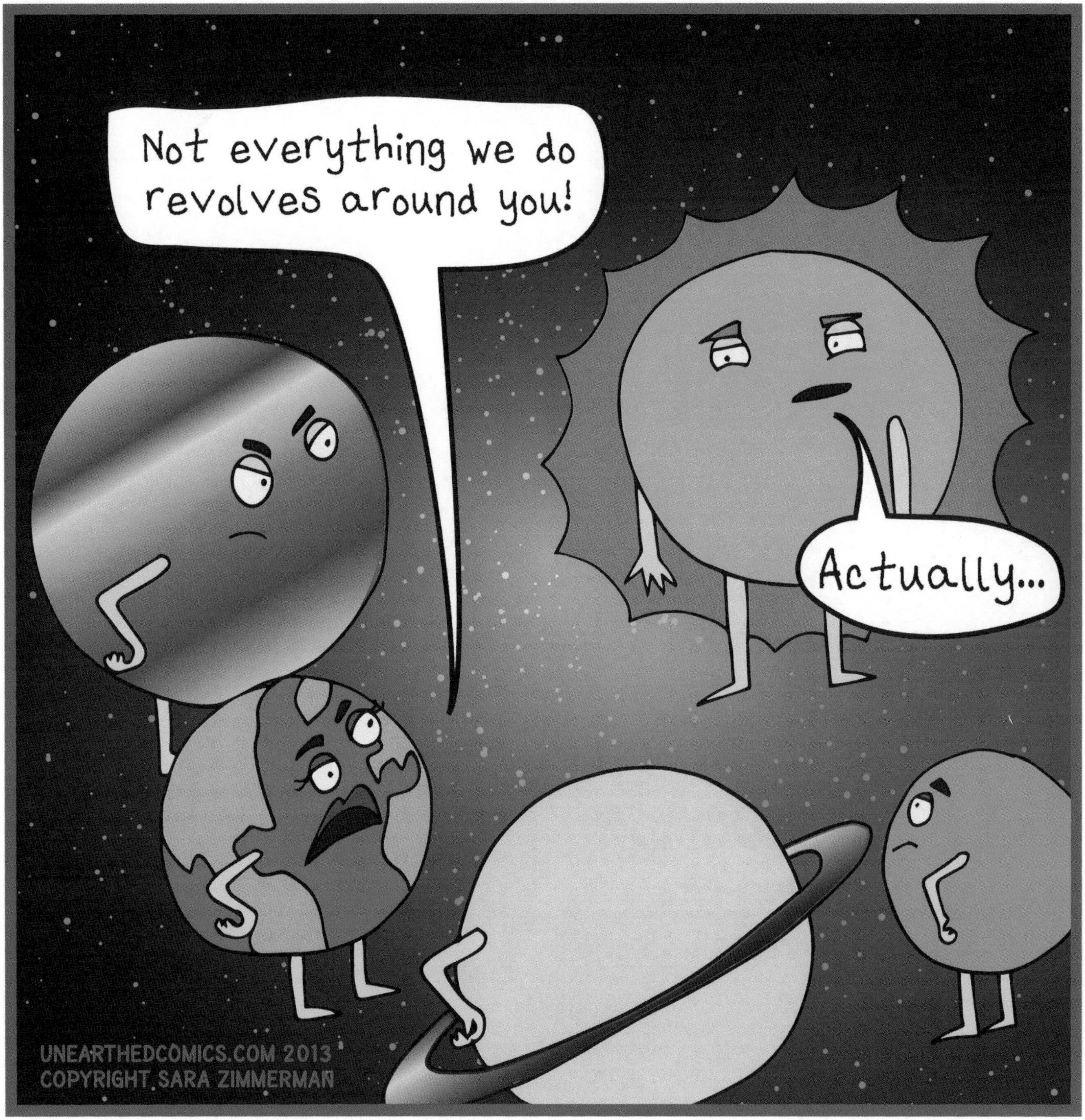
Not everything we do revolves around you!
Actually...
UNEARTHEDCOMICS.COM 2013
COPYRIGHT SARA ZIMMERMAN

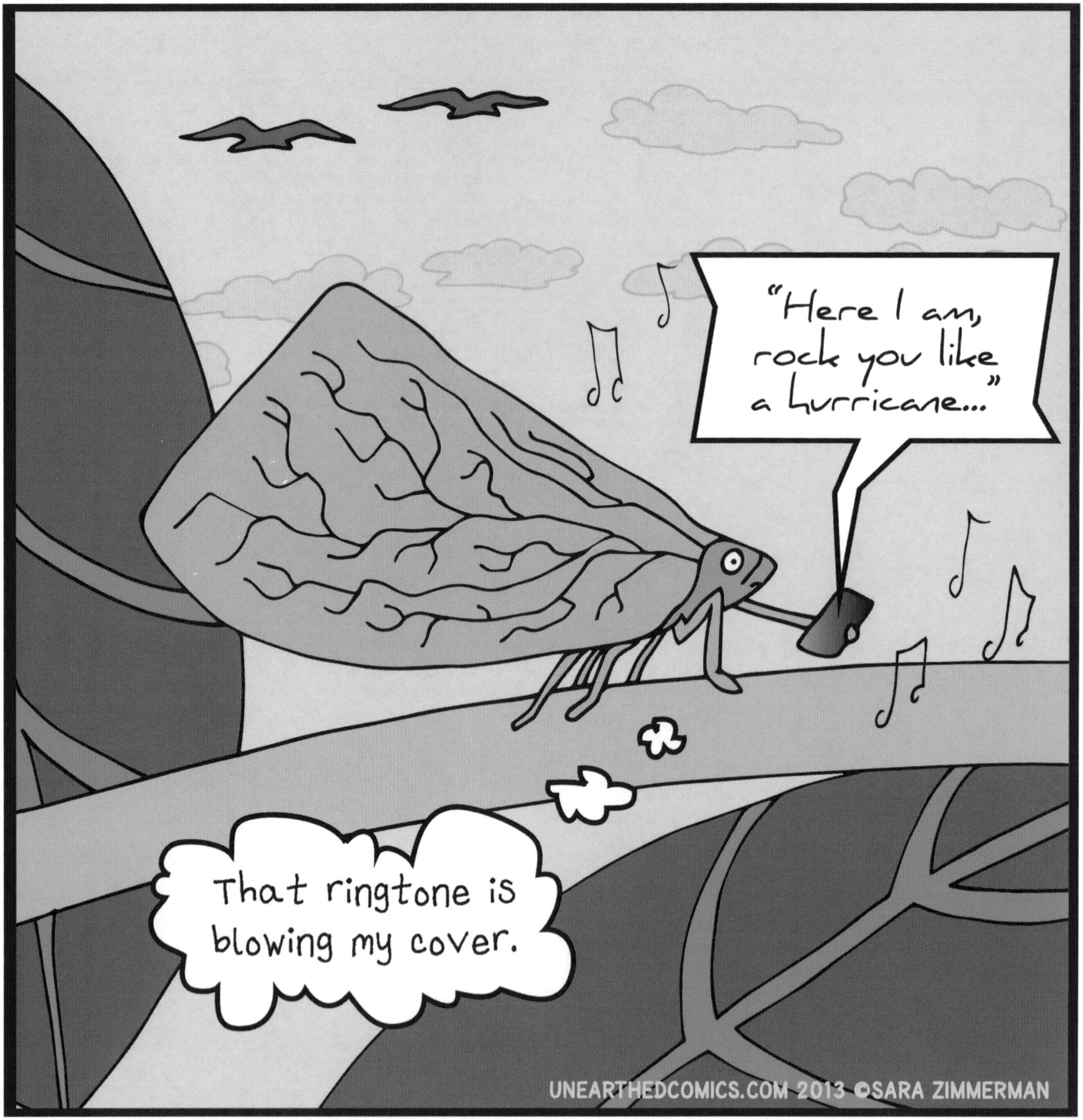
"Here I am, rock you like a hurricane..."
That ringtone is blowing my cover.
UNEARTHEDCOMICS.COM 2013 ©SARA ZIMMERMAN

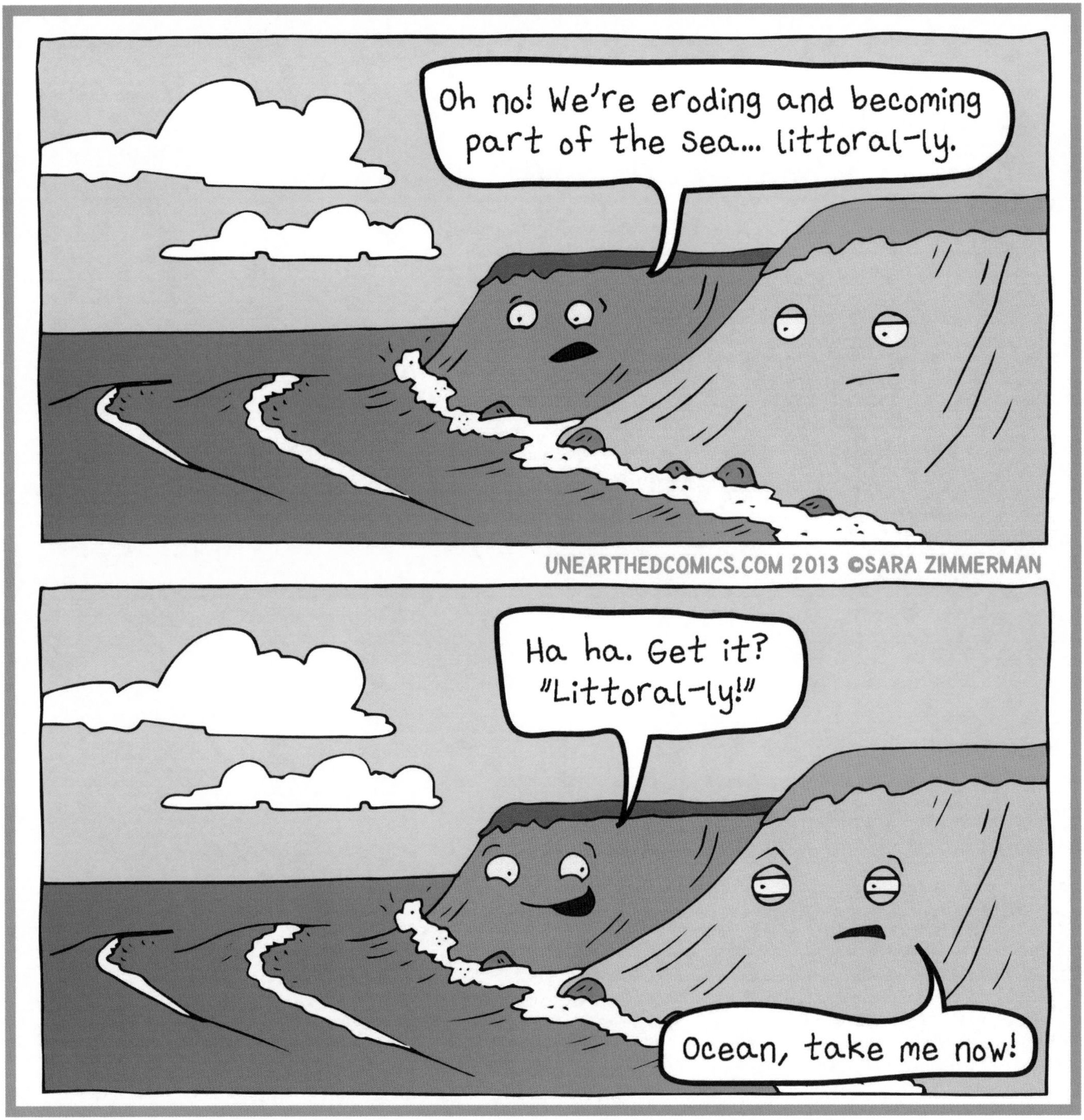
Oh no! We're eroding and becoming part of the sea... littoral-ly.
UNEARTHEDCOMICS.COM 2013 ©SARA ZIMMERMAN
Ha ha. Get it? "Littoral-ly!"
Ocean, take me now!

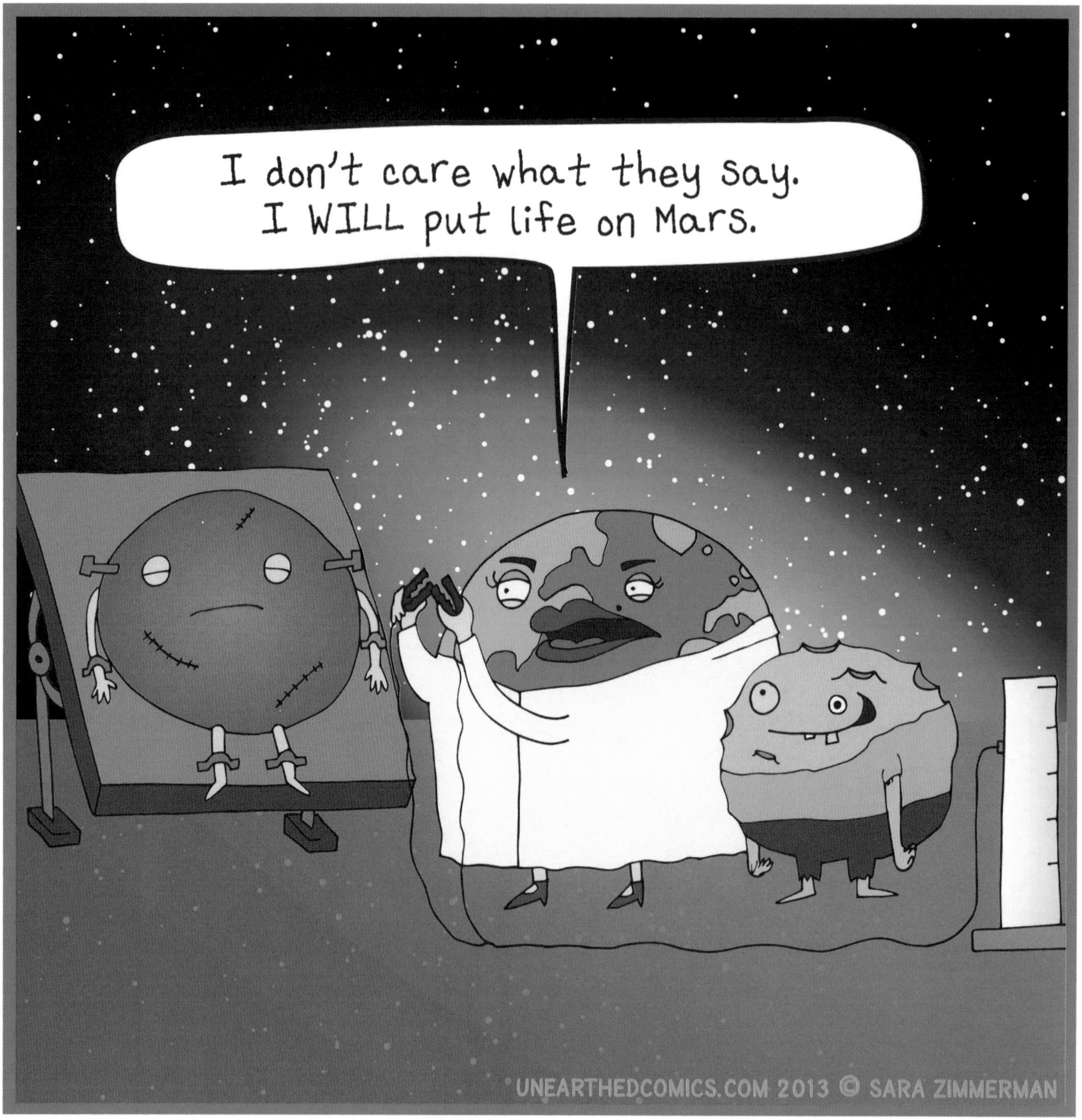
I don't care what they say.
I WILL put life on Mars.
UNEARTHEDCOMICS.COM 2013 © SARA ZIMMERMAN

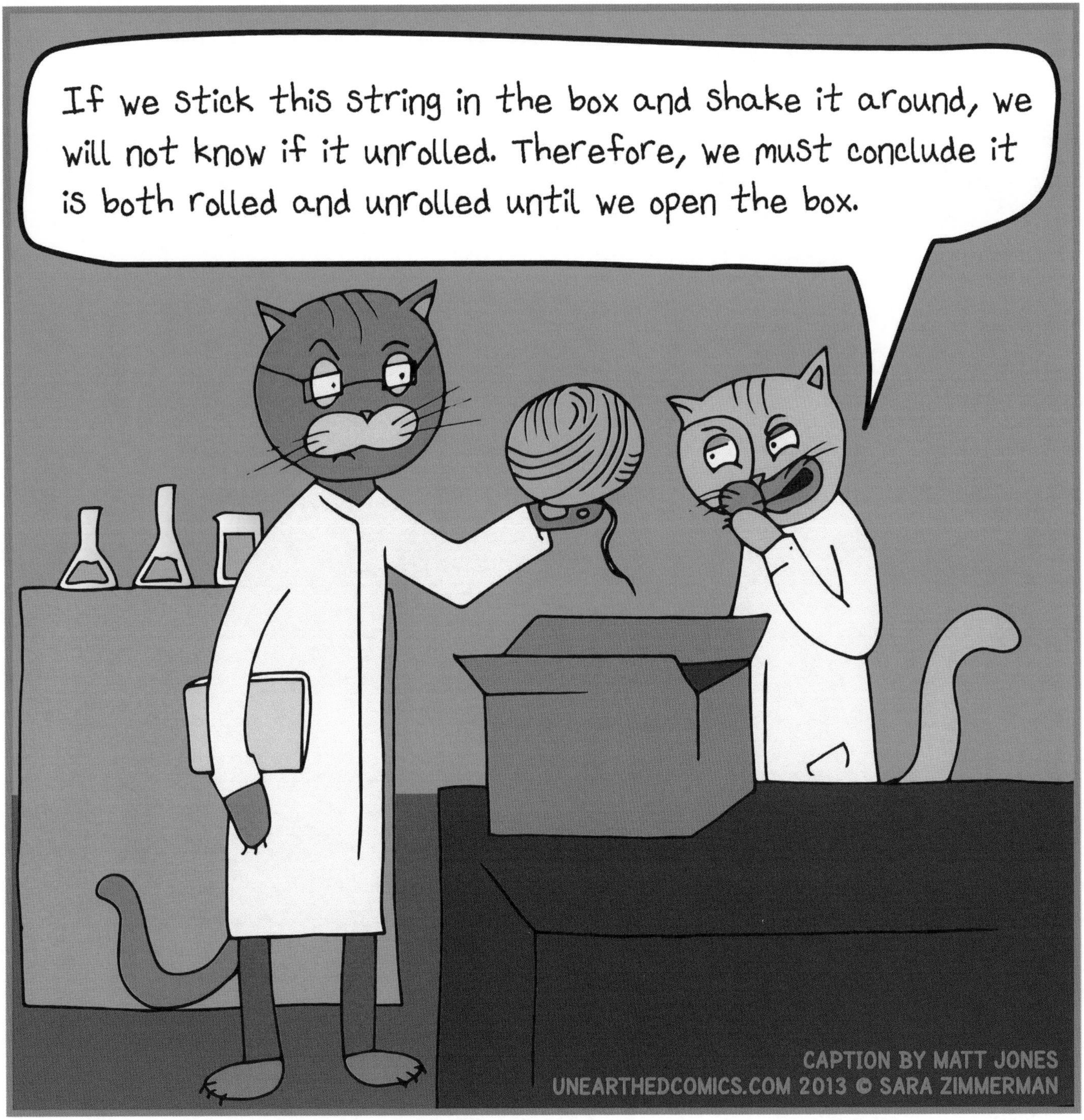
If we stick this string in the box and shake it around, we will not know if it unrolled. Therefore, we must conclude it is both rolled and unrolled until we open the box.
CAPTION BY MATT JONES
UNEARTHEDCOMICS.COM 2013 © SARA ZIMMERMAN

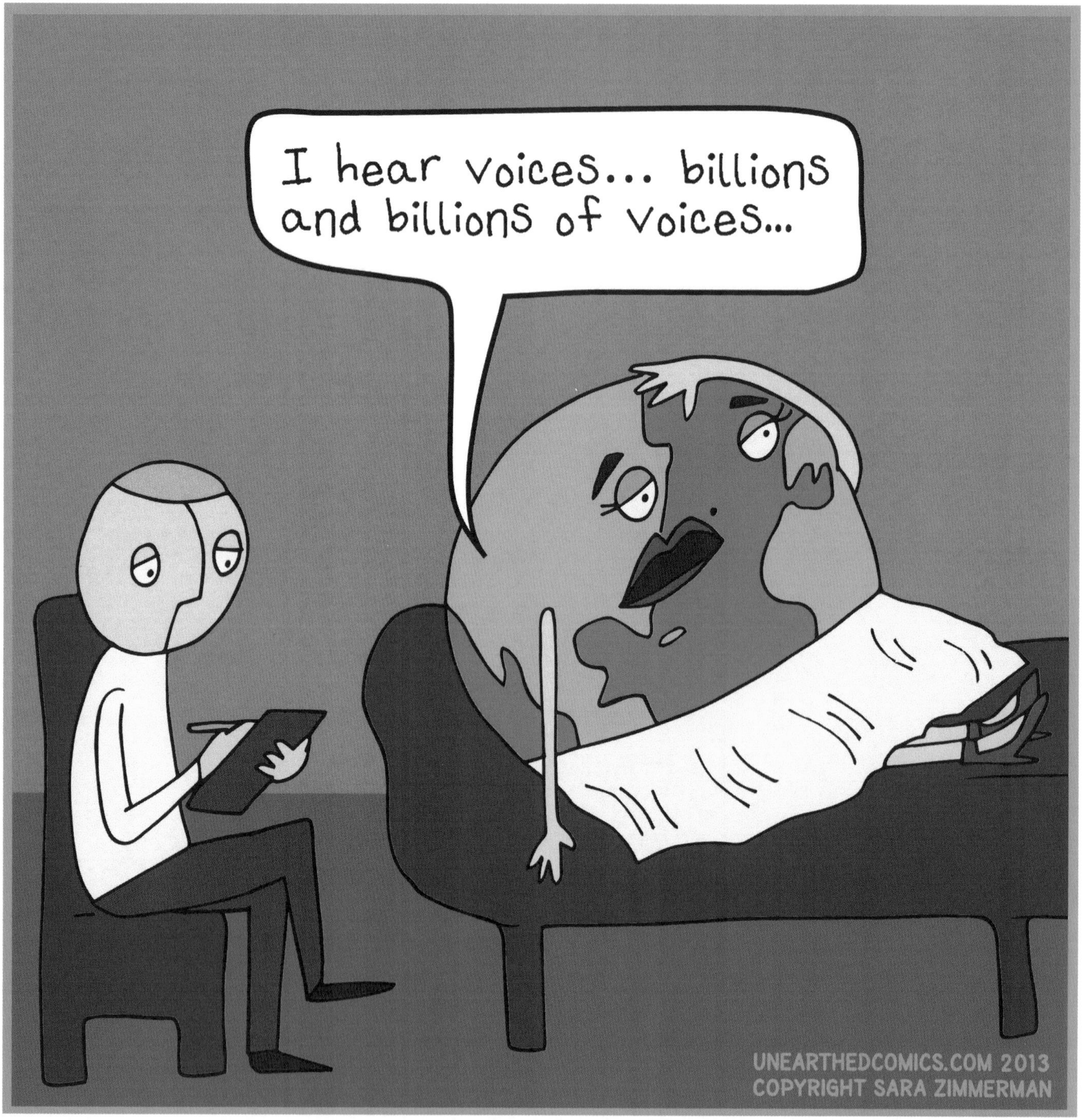
I hear voices... billions and billions of voices...
UNEARTHEDCOMICS.COM 2013
COPYRIGHT SARA ZIMMERMAN

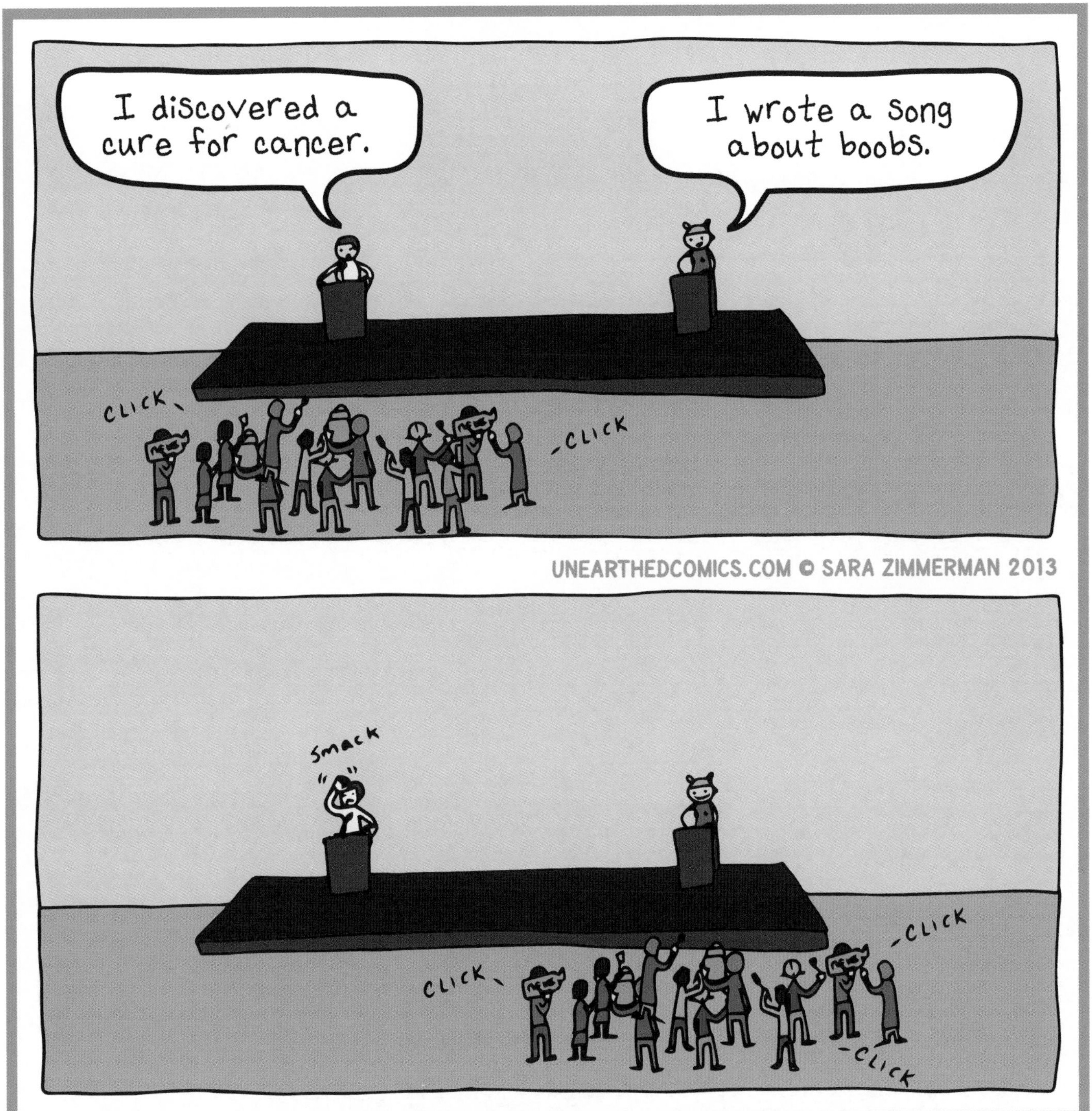
I discovered a cure for cancer.
I wrote a song about boobs.
CLICK
CLICK
UNEARTHEDCOMICS.COM © SARA ZIMMERMAN 2013
smack
CLICK
CLICK
CLICK

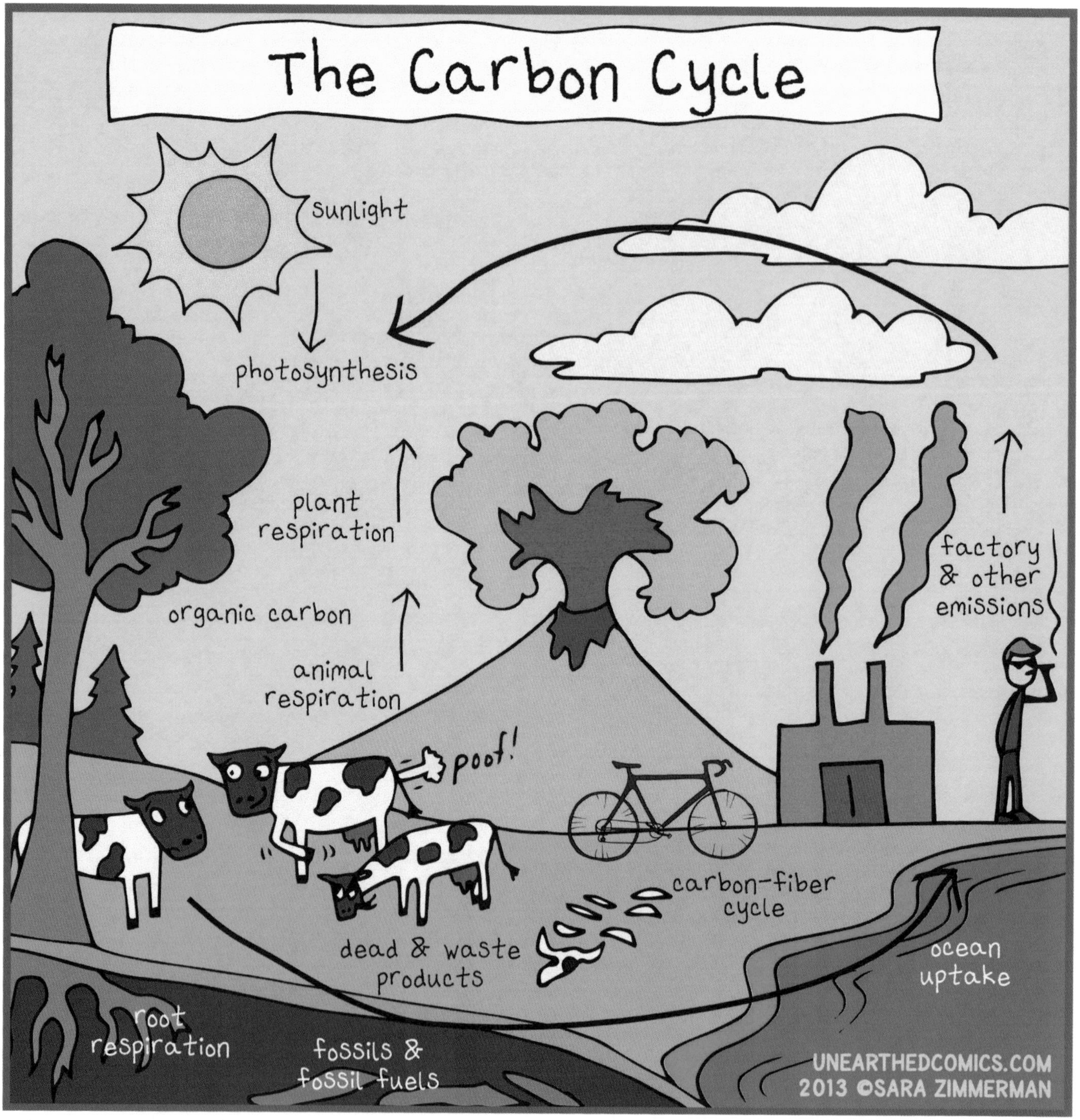
The Carbon Cycle
sunlight
photosynthesis
plant respiration
organic carbon
animal respiration
poof!
factory & other emissions
carbon-fiber cycle
dead & waste products
ocean uptake
root respiration
fossils & fossil fuels
UNEARTHEDCOMICS.COM
2013 ©SARA ZIMMERMAN

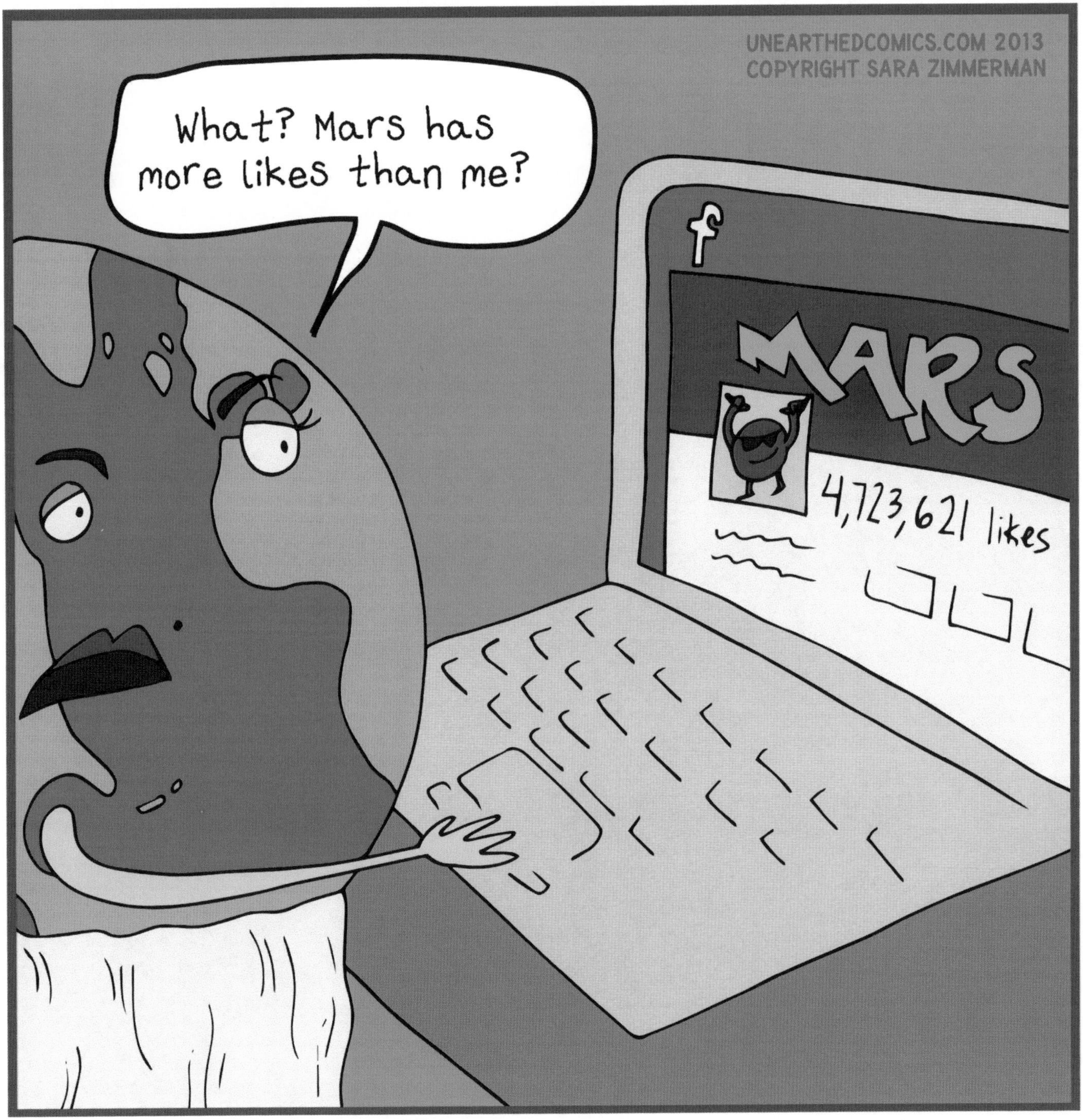

UNEARTHEDCOMICS.COM 2013
COPYRIGHT SARA ZIMMERMAN
What? Mars has more likes than me?
f
MARS
4,723,621 likes

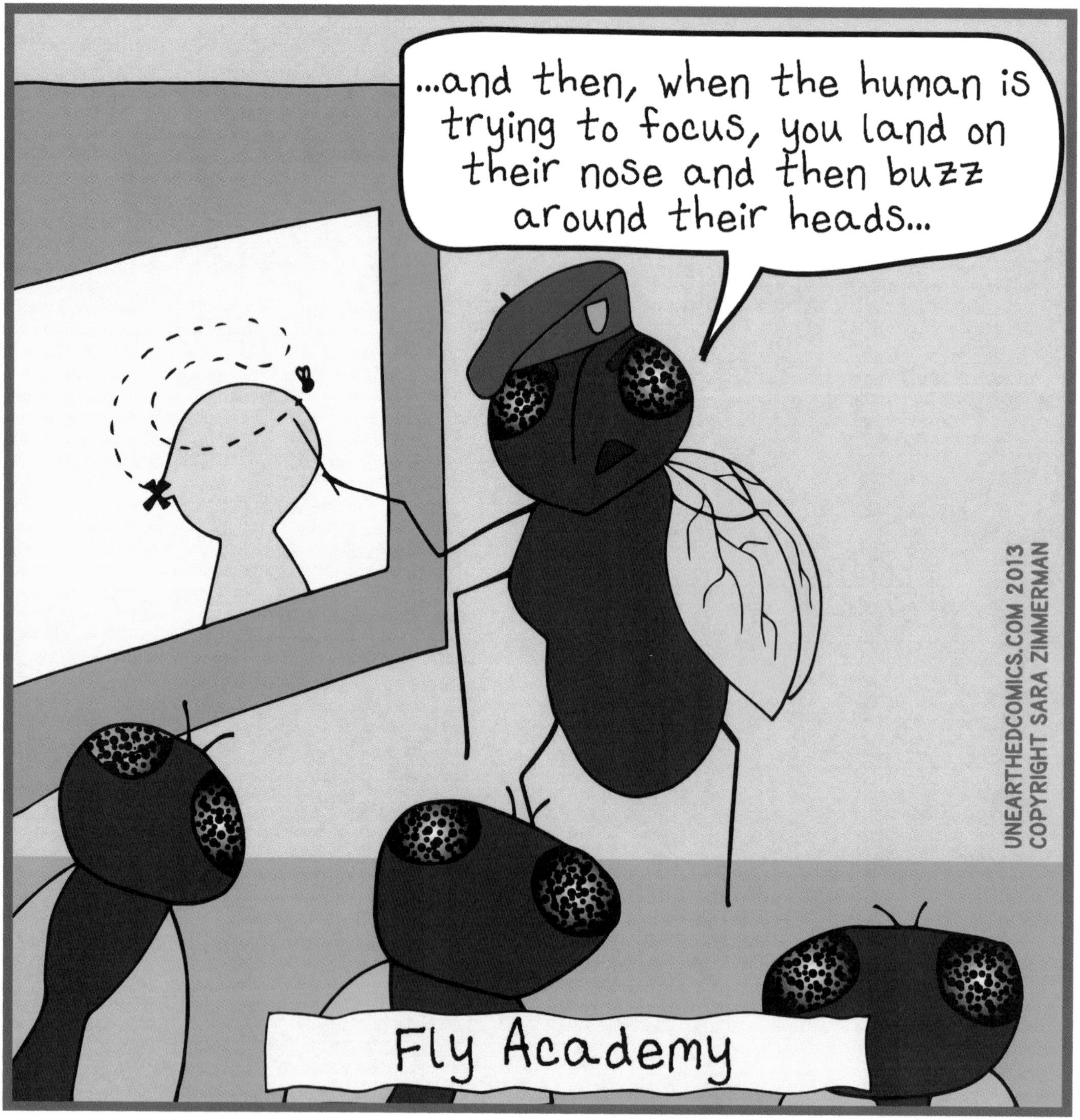
...and then, when the human is trying to focus, you land on their nose and then buzz around their heads...
Fly Academy
UNEARTHEDCOMICS.COM 2013
COPYRIGHT SARA ZIMMERMAN

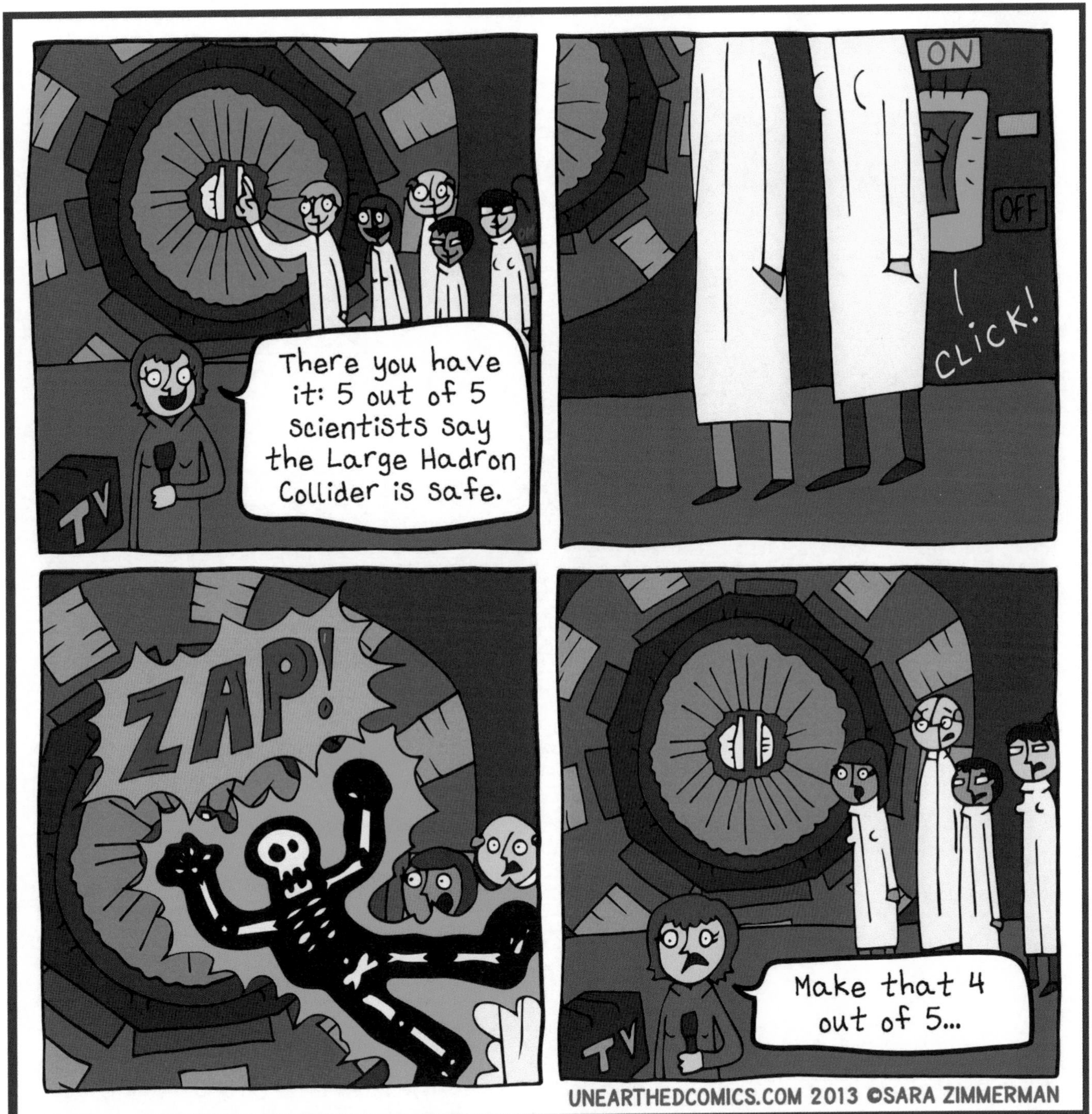
There you have it: 5 out of 5 scientists say the Large Hadron Collider is safe.
TV
ON
OFF
CLICK!
ZAP!
Make that 4 out of 5...
TV
UNEARTHEDCOMICS.COM 2013 ©SARA ZIMMERMAN

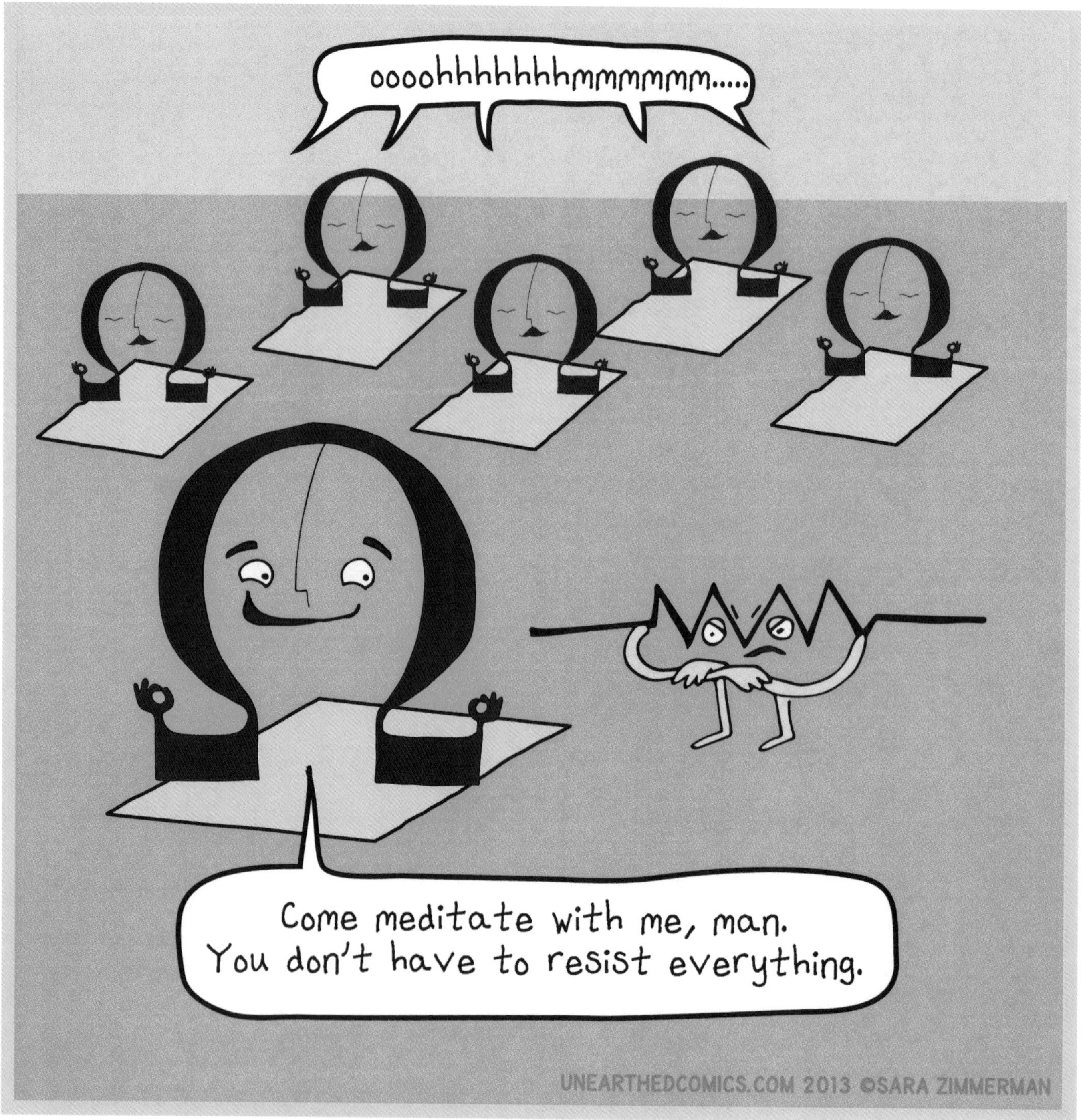
oooohhhhhhhmmmmmm.....
Come meditate with me, man. You don't have to resist everything.
UNEARTHEDCOMICS.COM 2013 ©SARA ZIMMERMAN

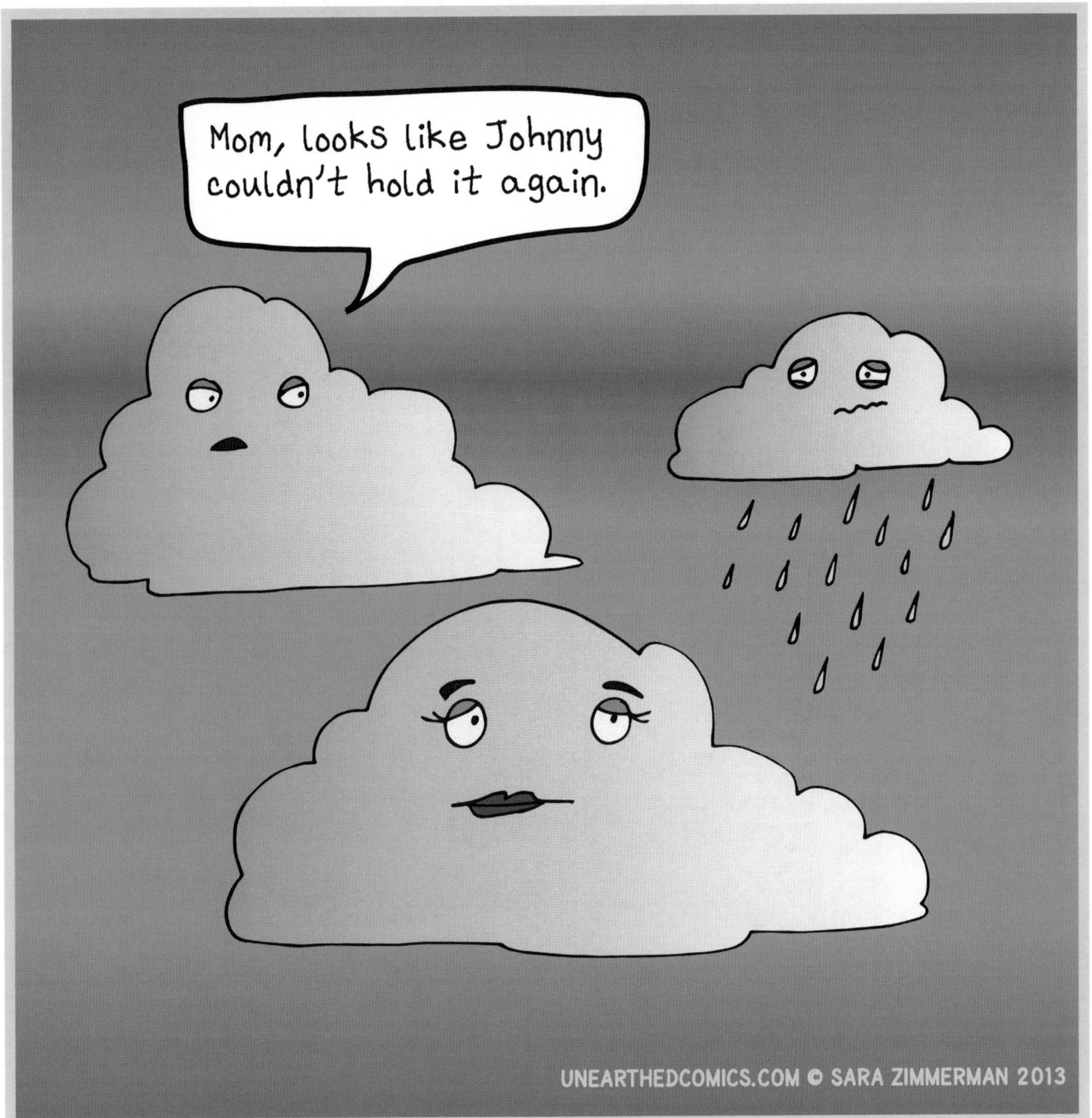
Mom, looks like Johnny couldn't hold it again.
UNEARTHEDCOMICS.COM © SARA ZIMMERMAN 2013

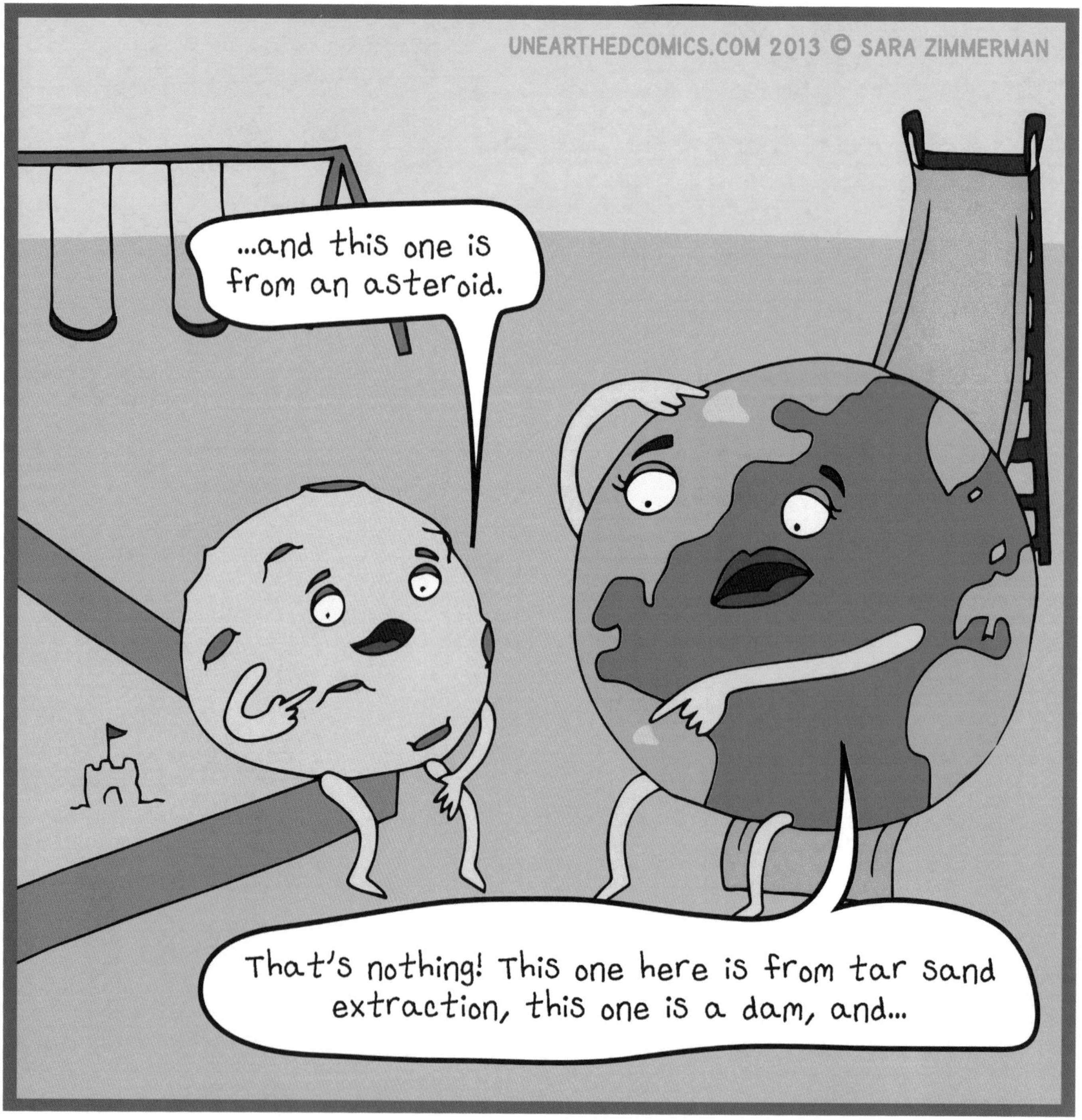
UNEARTHEDCOMICS.COM 2013 © SARA ZIMMERMAN
...and this one is from an asteroid.
That's nothing! This one here is from tar sand extraction, this one is a dam, and...

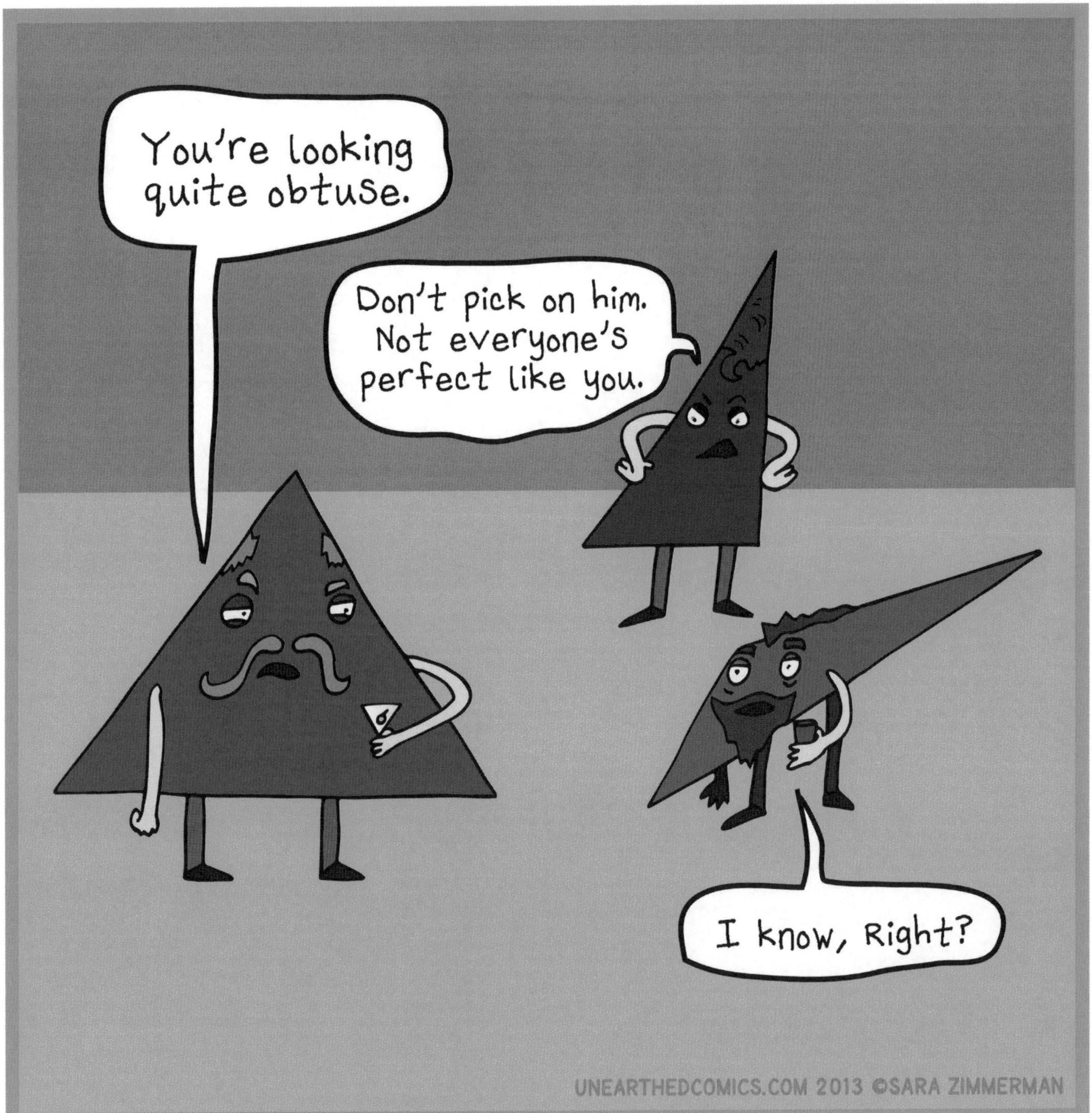
You're looking quite obtuse.
Don't pick on him. Not everyone's perfect like you.
I know, Right?
UNEARTHEDCOMICS.COM 2013 ©SARA ZIMMERMAN

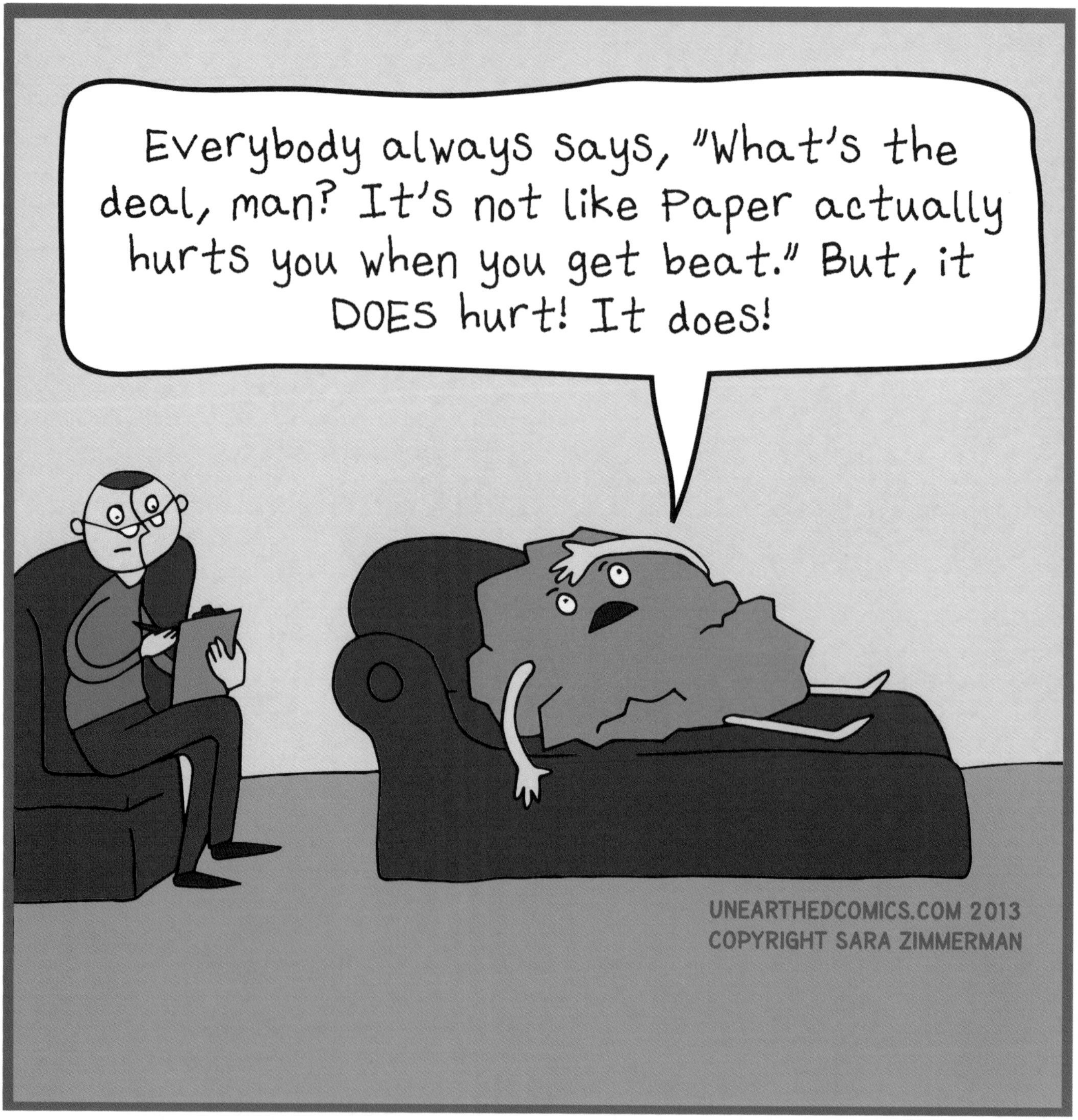
Everybody always says, "What's the deal, man? It's not like Paper actually hurts you when you get beat." But, it DOES hurt! It does!
UNEARTHEDCOMICS.COM 2013
COPYRIGHT SARA ZIMMERMAN

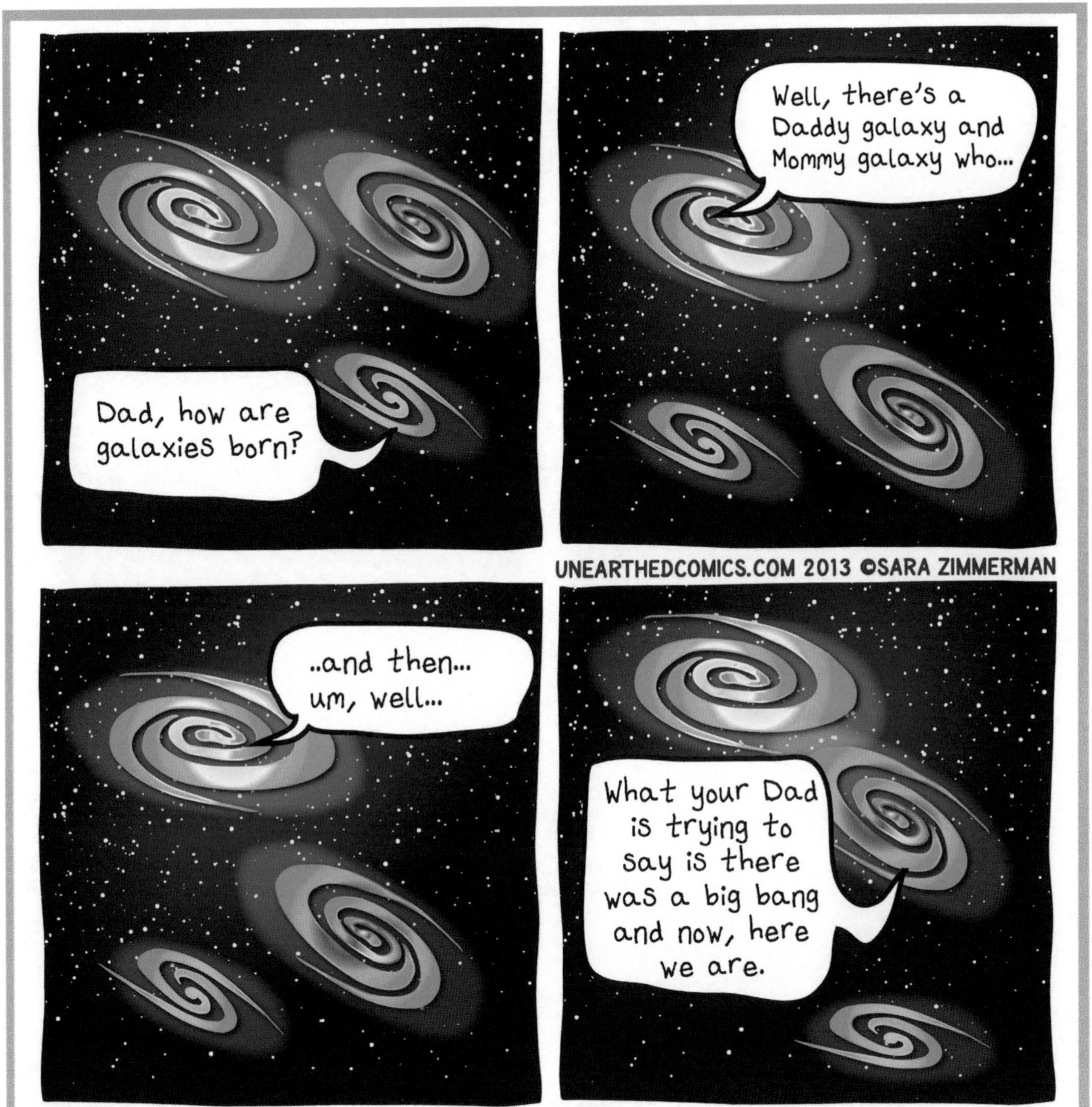
Dad, how are galaxies born?
Well, there's a Daddy galaxy and Mommy galaxy who...
UNEARTHEDCOMICS.COM 2013 ©SARA ZIMMERMAN
..and then... um, well...
What your Dad is trying to say is there was a big bang and now, here we are.

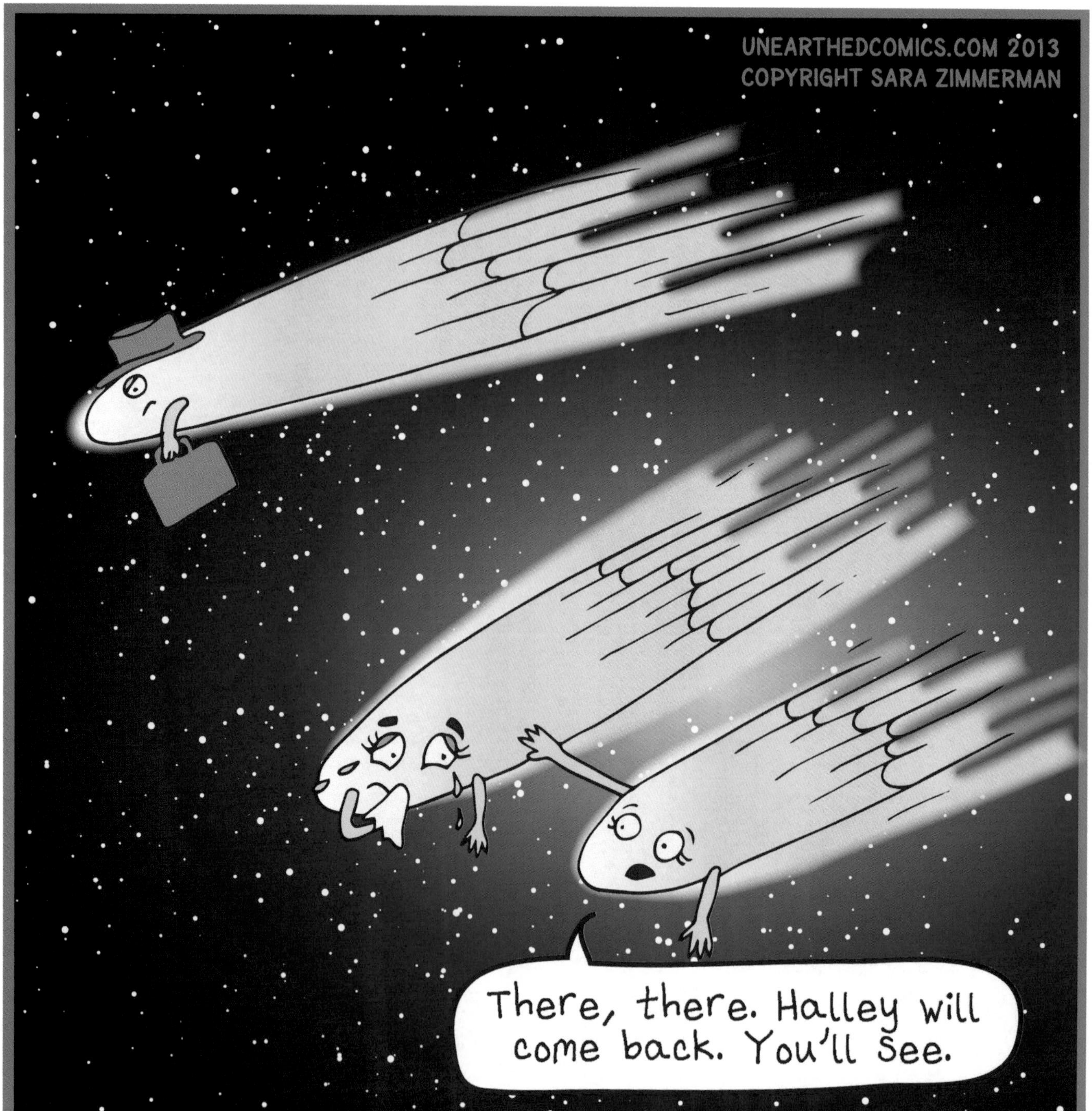
UNEARTHEDCOMICS.COM 2013
COPYRIGHT SARA ZIMMERMAN
There, there. Halley will come back. You'll See.

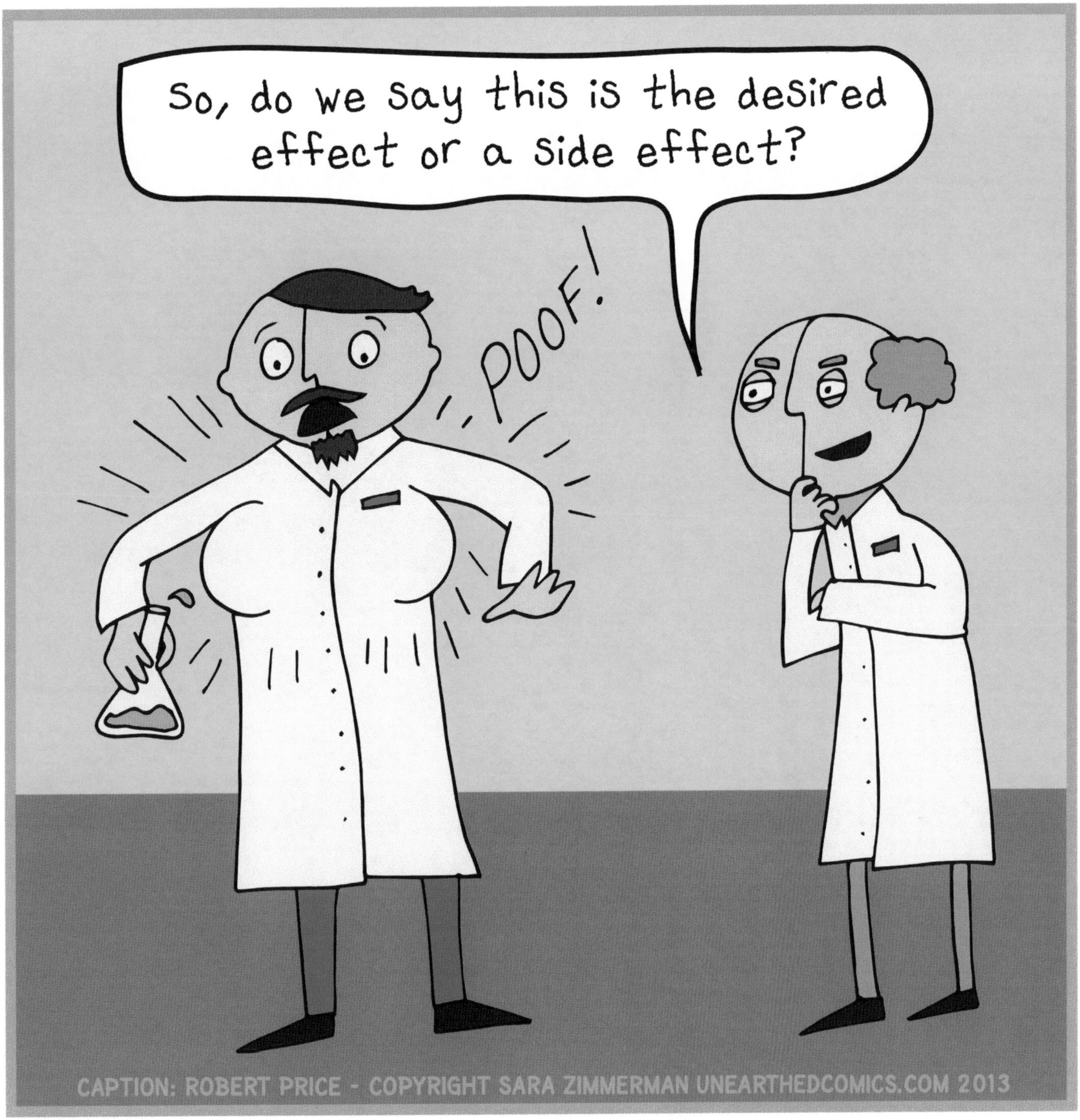
So, do we say this is the desired effect or a side effect?
POOF!
CAPTION: ROBERT PRICE - COPYRIGHT SARA ZIMMERMAN UNEARTHEDCOMICS.COM 2013

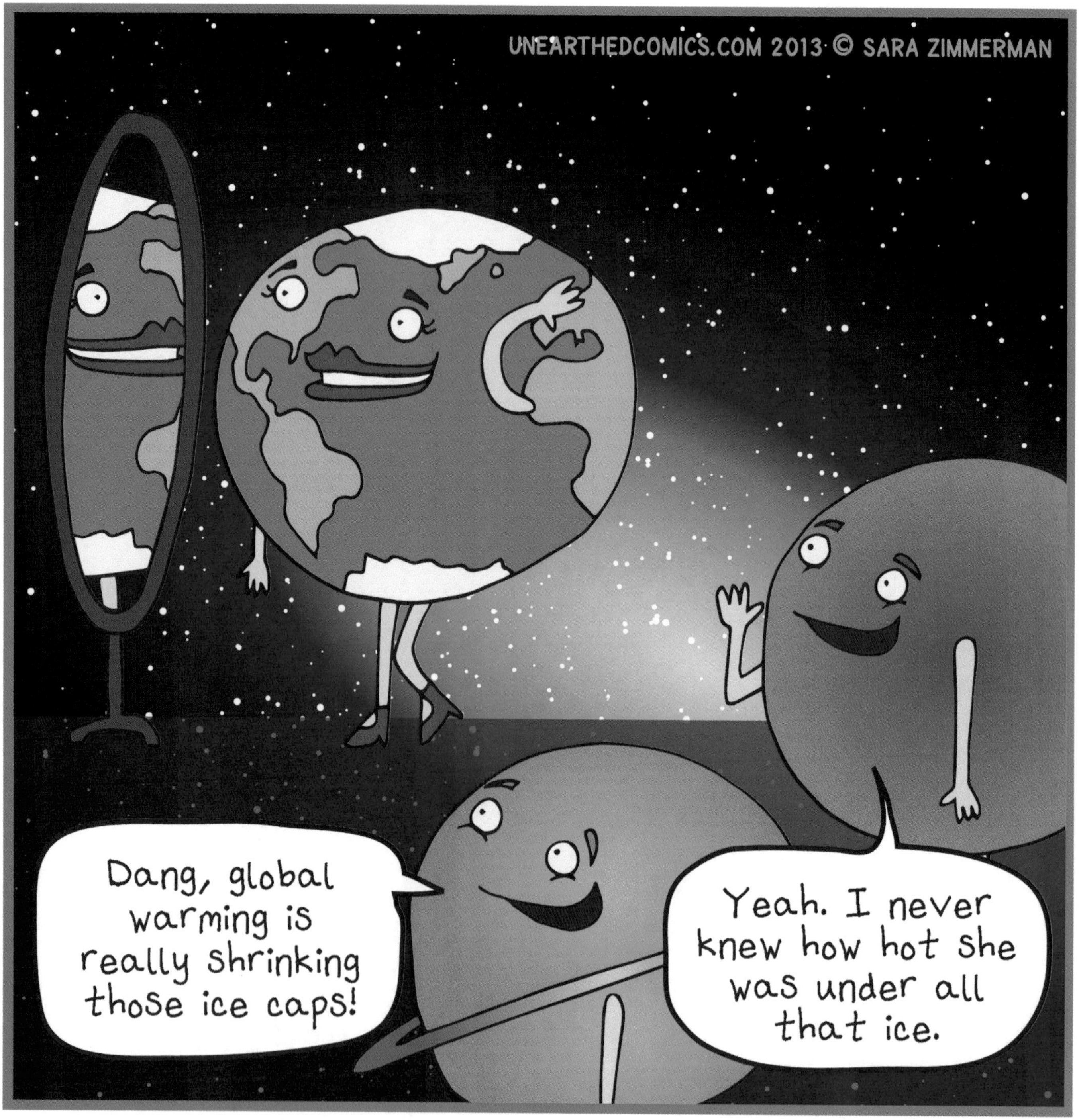
UNEARTHEDCOMICS.COM 2013 © SARA ZIMMERMAN
Dang, global warming is really shrinking those ice caps!
Yeah. I never knew how hot she was under all that ice.

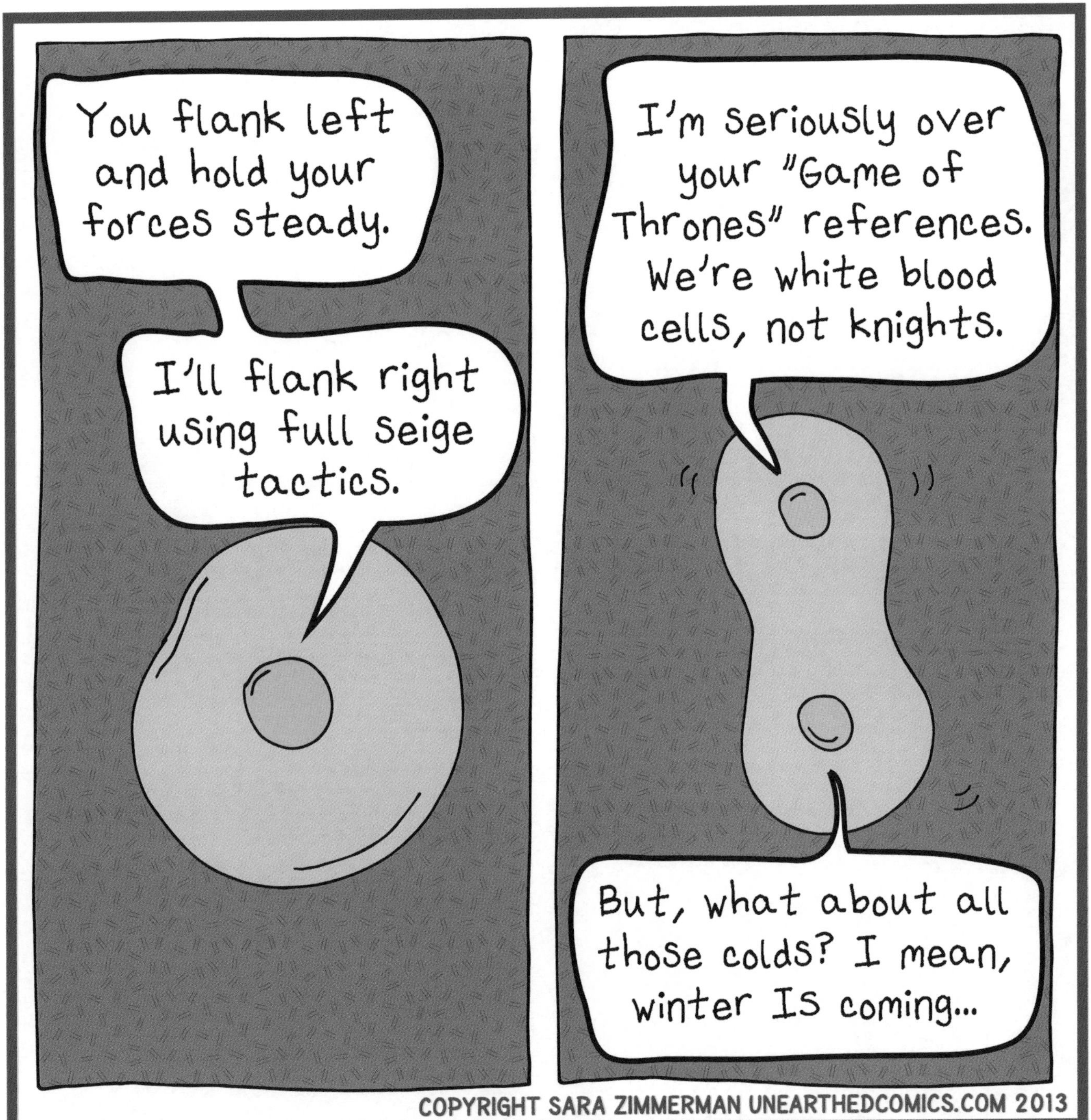
You flank left and hold your forces steady.
I'll flank right using full seige tactics.
I'm seriously over your "Game of Thrones" references. We're white blood cells, not knights.
But, what about all those colds? I mean, winter IS coming...

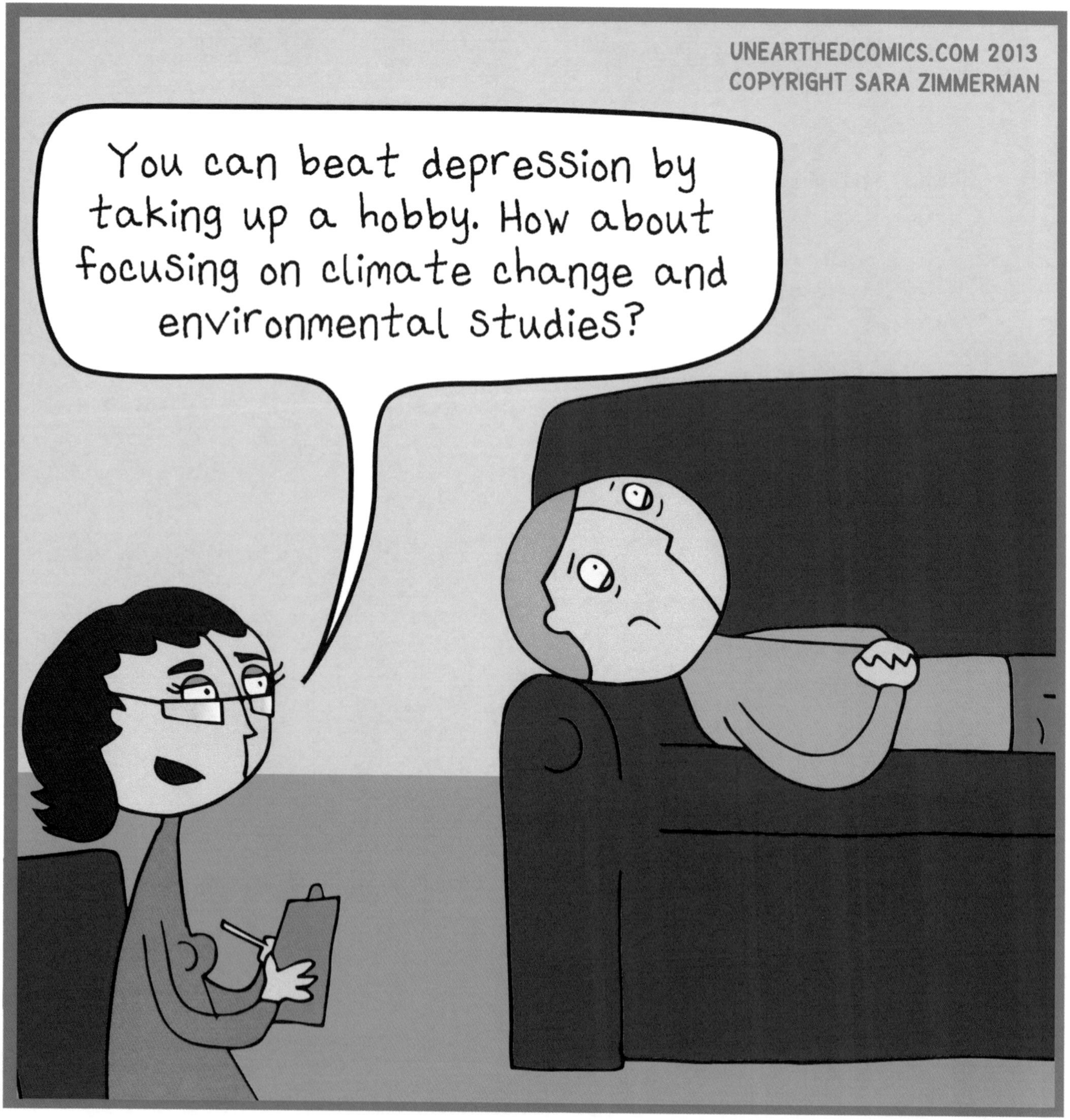
UNEARTHEDCOMICS.COM 2013
COPYRIGHT SARA ZIMMERMAN
You can beat depression by taking up a hobby. How about focusing on climate change and environmental studies?

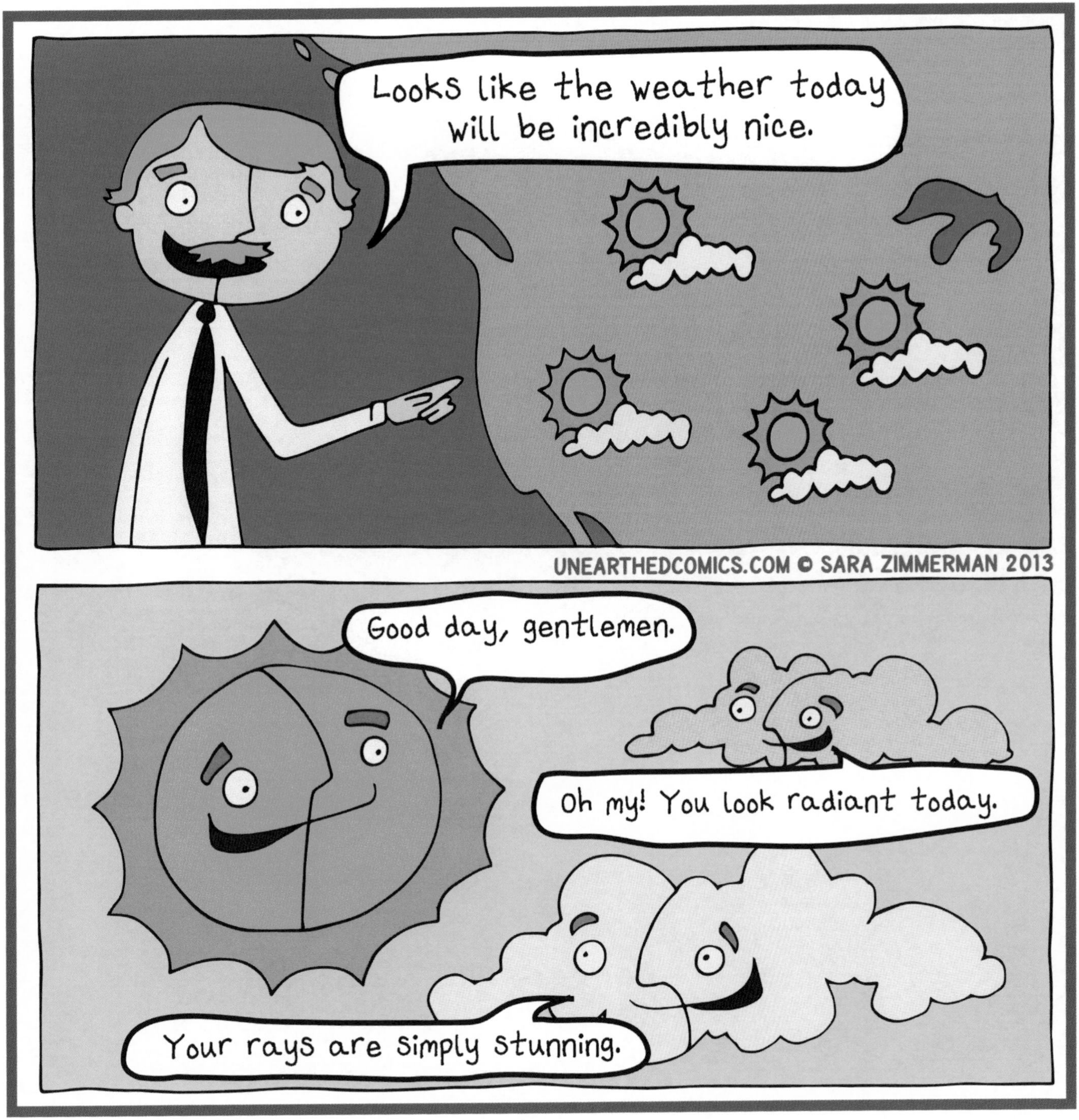
Looks like the weather today will be incredibly nice.
UNEARTHEDCOMICS.COM © SARA ZIMMERMAN 2013
Good day, gentlemen.
Oh my! You look radiant today.
Your rays are simply stunning.

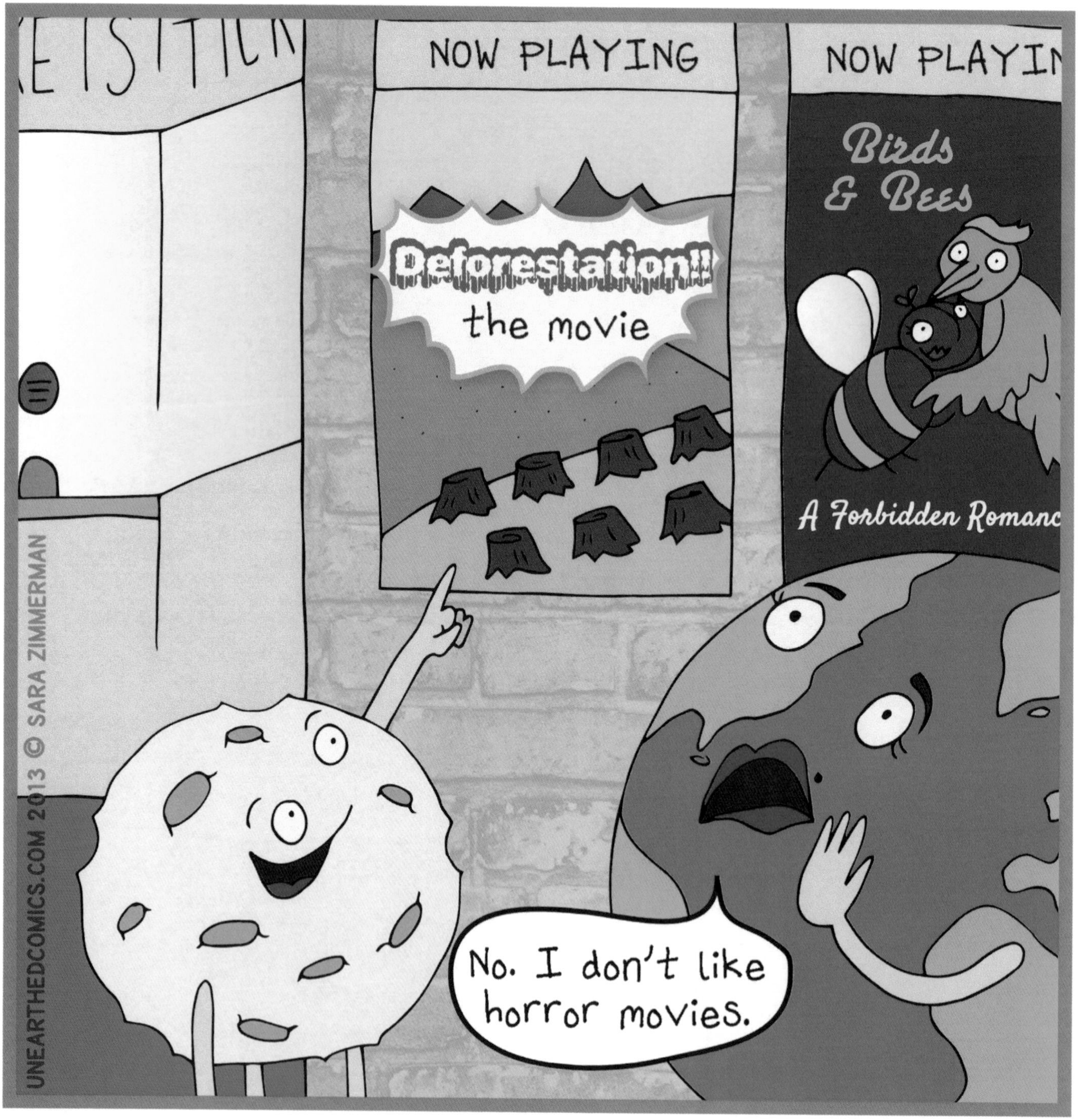
NOW PLAYING
Deforestation!!
the movie
NOW PLAYIN
Birds
& Bees
A Forbidden Romanc
UNEARTHEDCOMICS.COM 2013 © SARA ZIMMERMAN
No. I don't like horror movies.

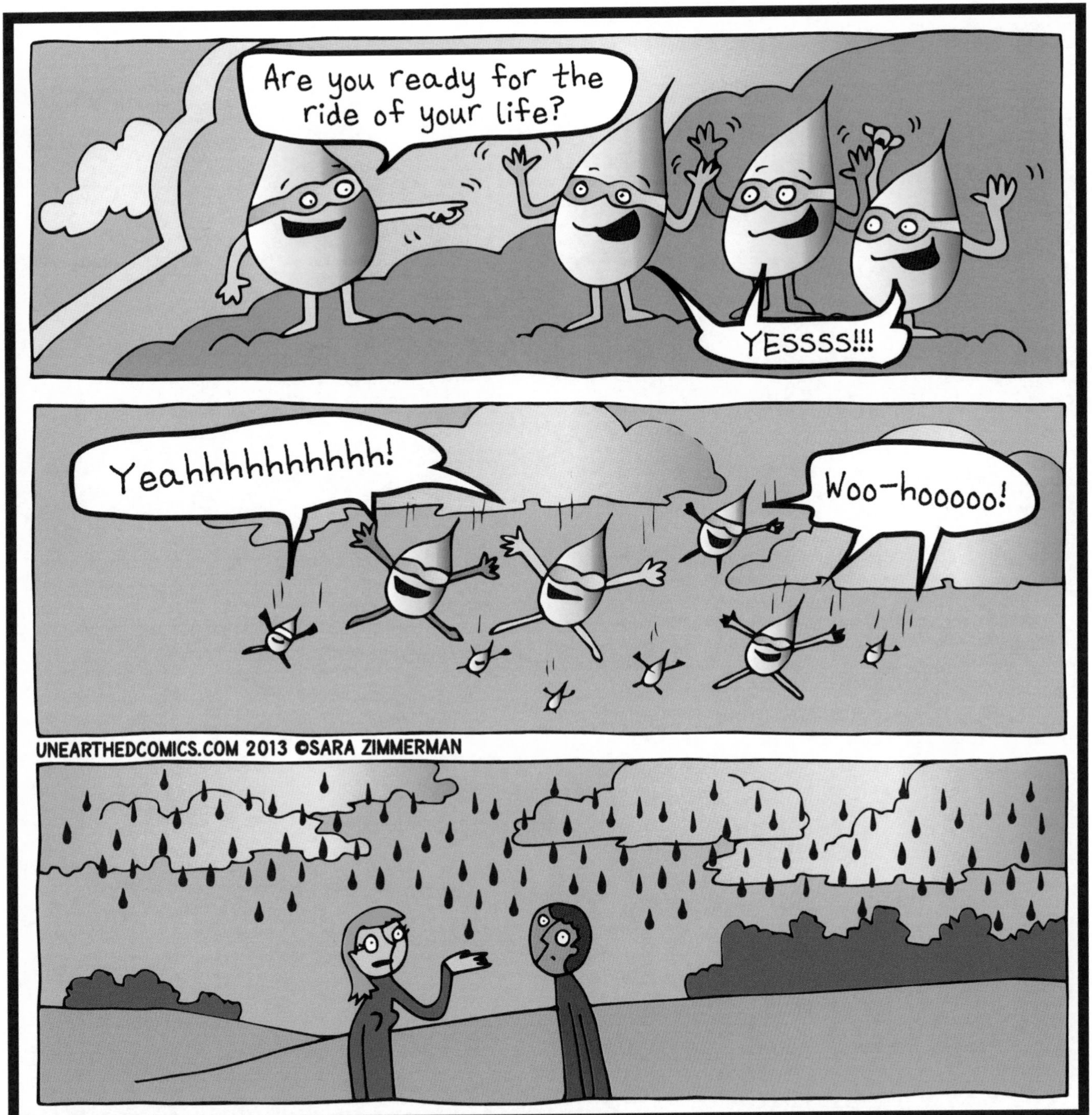
Are you ready for the ride of your life?
YESSSS!!!
Yeahhhhhhhhhh!
Woo-hoooooo!
UNEARTHEDCOMICS.COM 2013 ©SARA ZIMMERMAN

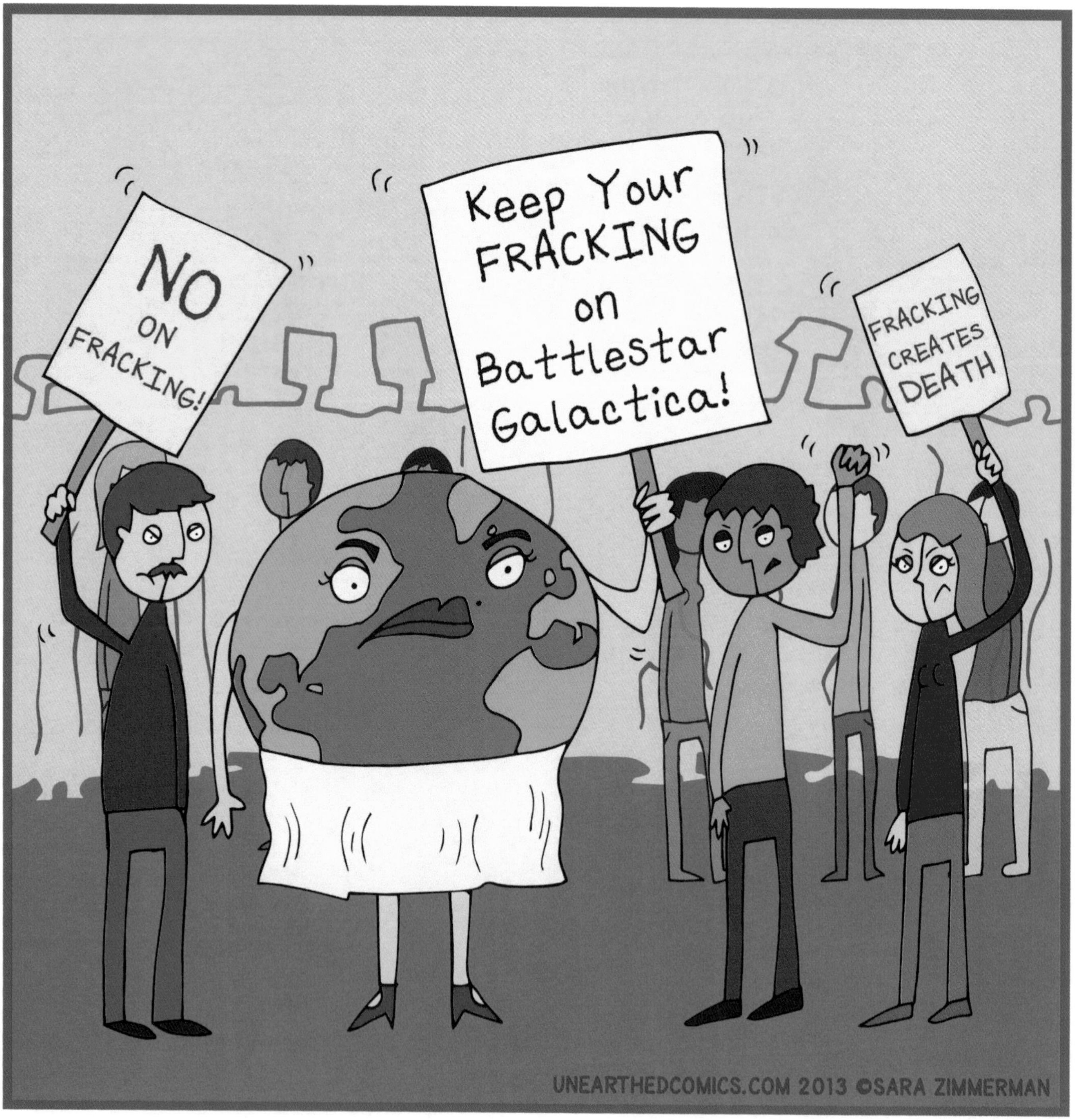
NO
ON
FRACKING!
Keep Your
FRACKING
on
Battlestar
Galactica!
FRACKING
CREATES
DEATH
UNEARTHEDCOMICS.COM 2013 ©SARA ZIMMERMAN

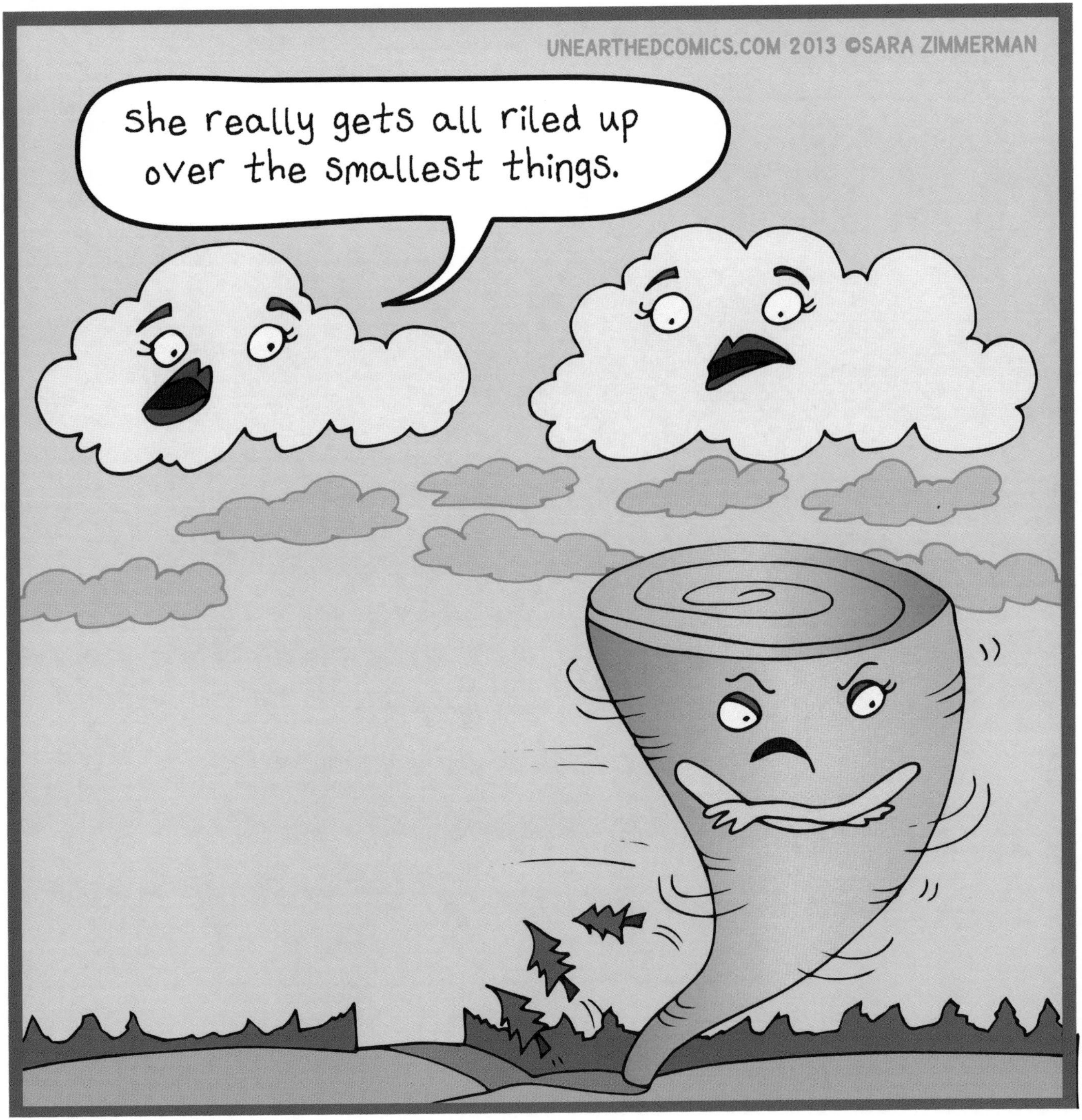
UNEARTHEDCOMICS.COM 2013 ©SARA ZIMMERMAN
she really gets all riled up over the smallest things.

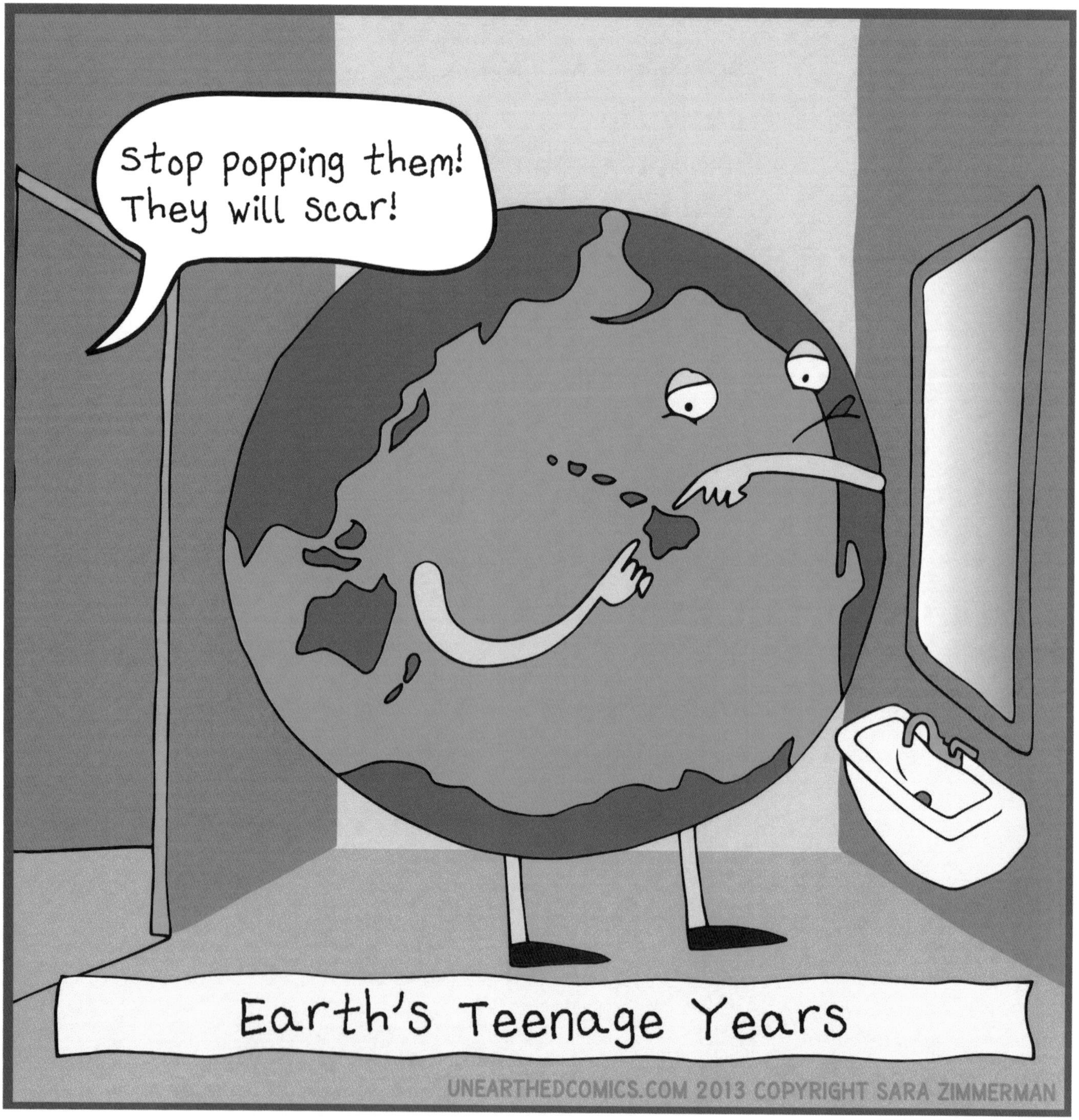
Stop popping them! They will scar!
Earth's Teenage Years
UNEARTHEDCOMICS.COM 2013 COPYRIGHT SARA ZIMMERMAN

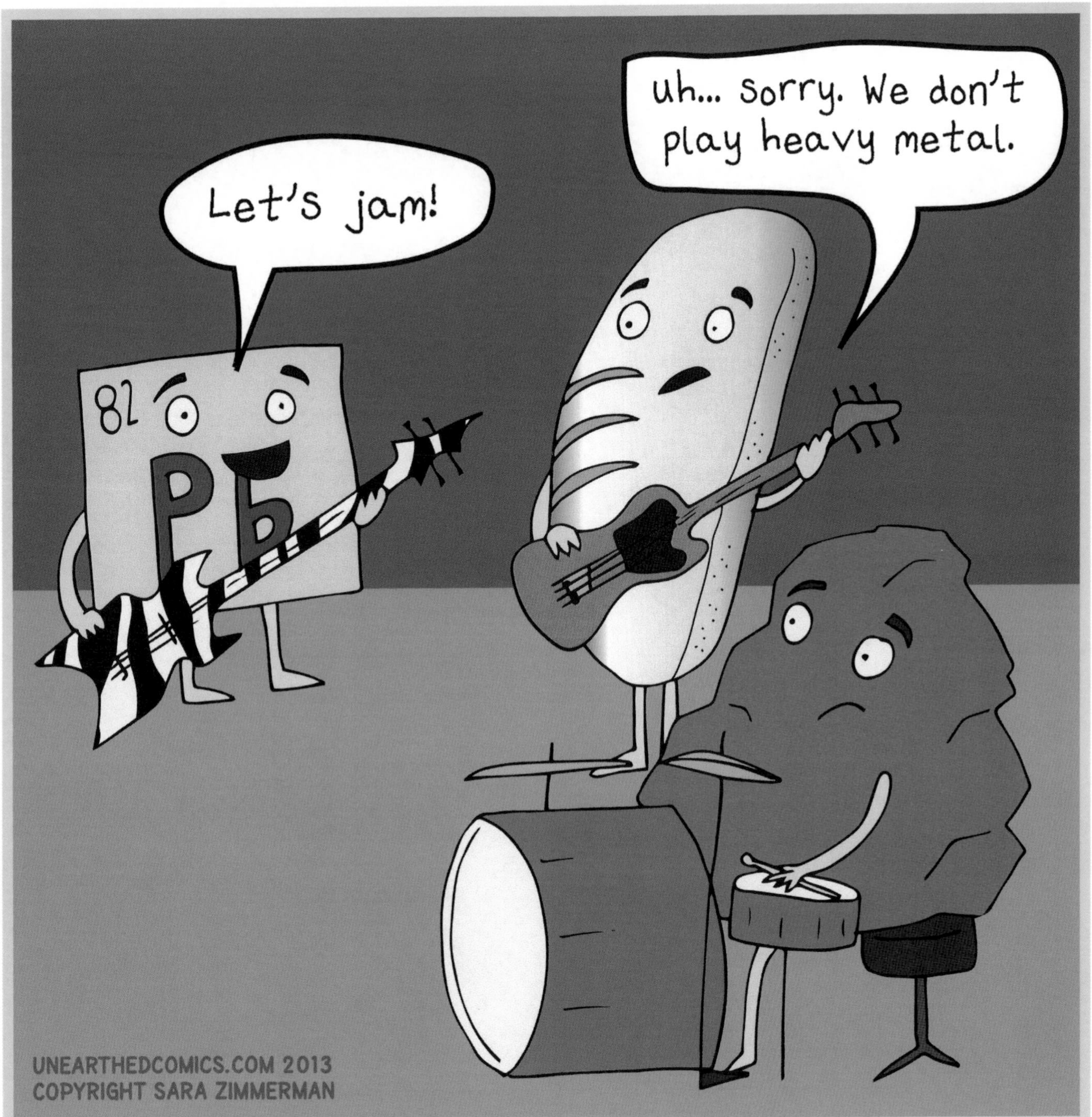
Let's jam!
uh... sorry. We don't play heavy metal.
82
Pb
UNEARTHEDCOMICS.COM 2013
COPYRIGHT SARA ZIMMERMAN

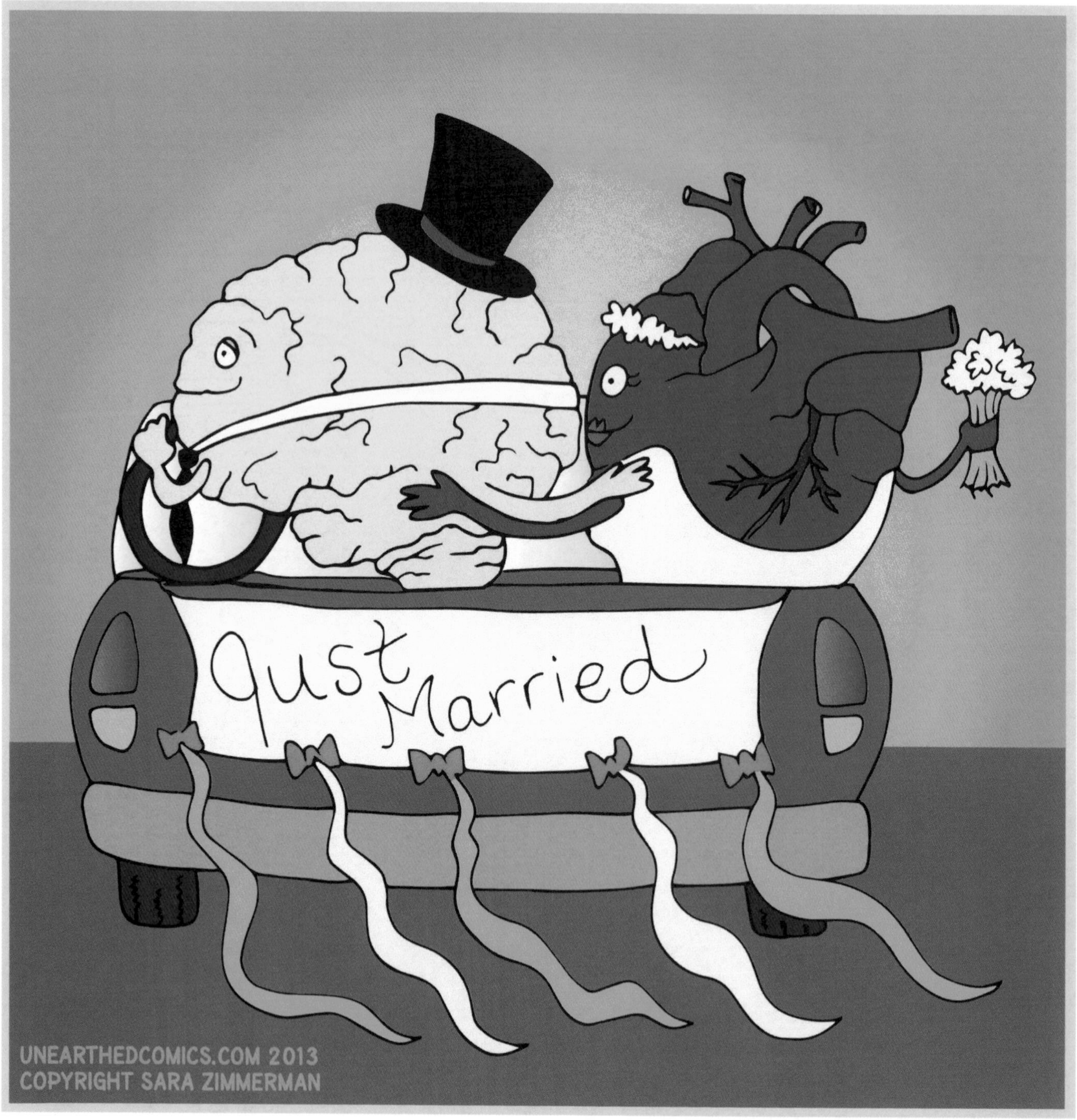
Just Married
UNEARTHEDCOMICS.COM 2013
COPYRIGHT SARA ZIMMERMAN

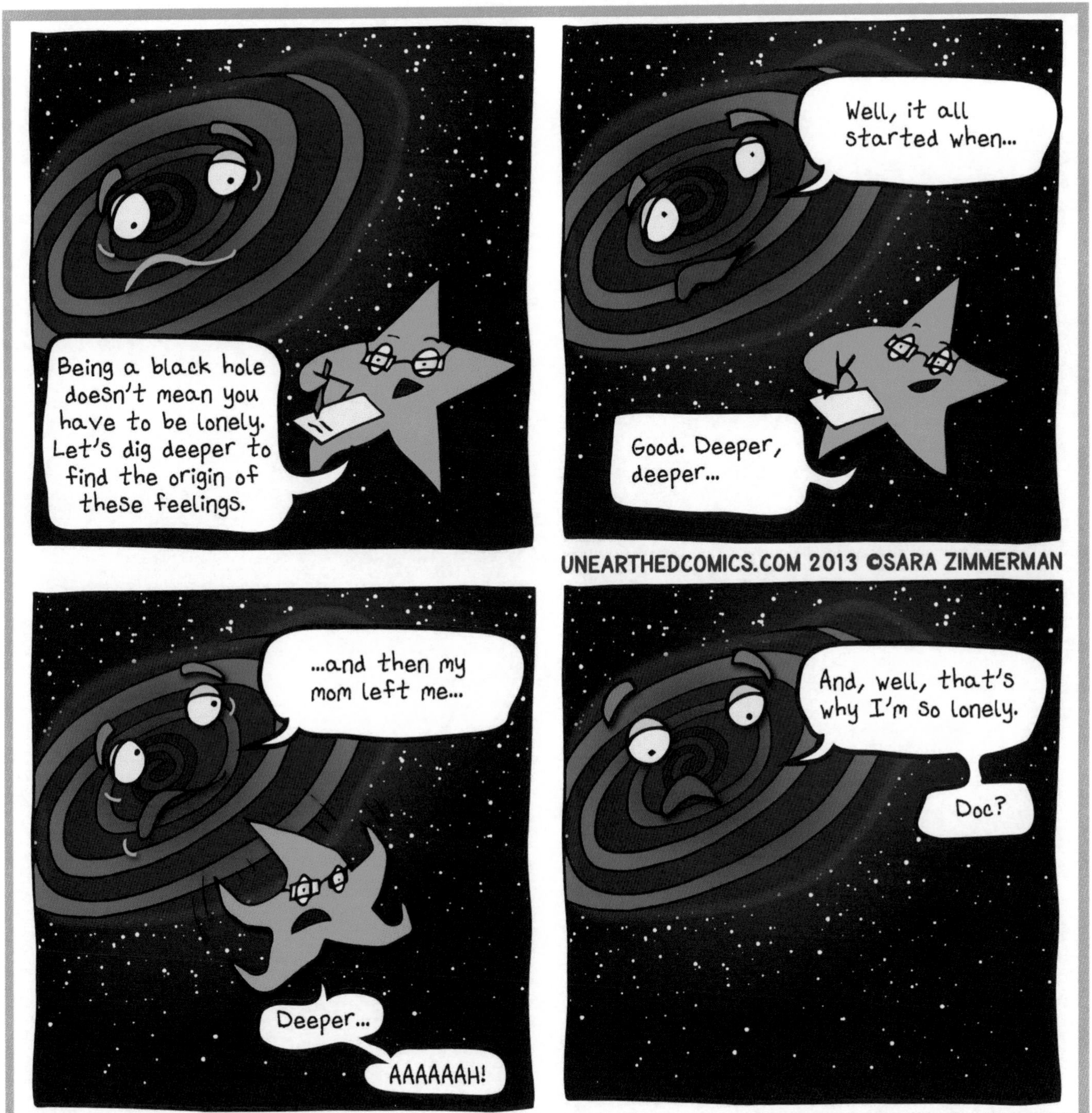
Being a black hole doesn't mean you have to be lonely. Let's dig deeper to find the origin of these feelings.
Well, it all started when...
Good. Deeper, deeper...
UNEARTHEDCOMICS.COM 2013 ©SARA ZIMMERMAN
...and then my mom left me...
Deeper...
AAAAAAH!
And, well, that's why I'm so lonely.
Doc?

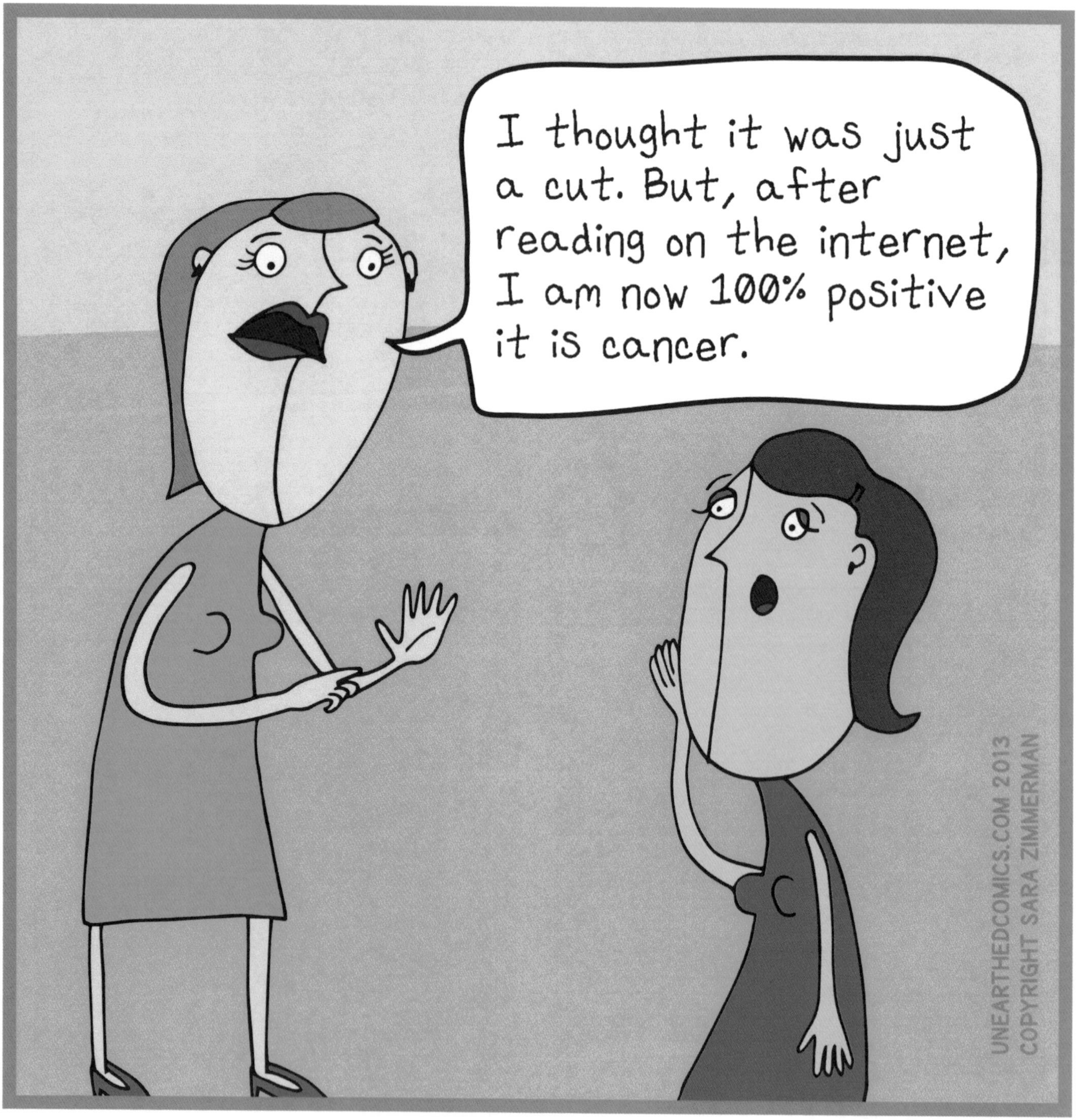
I thought it was just a cut. But, after reading on the internet, I am now 100% positive it is cancer.
UNEARTHEDCOMICS.COM 2013
COPYRIGHT SARA ZIMMERMAN

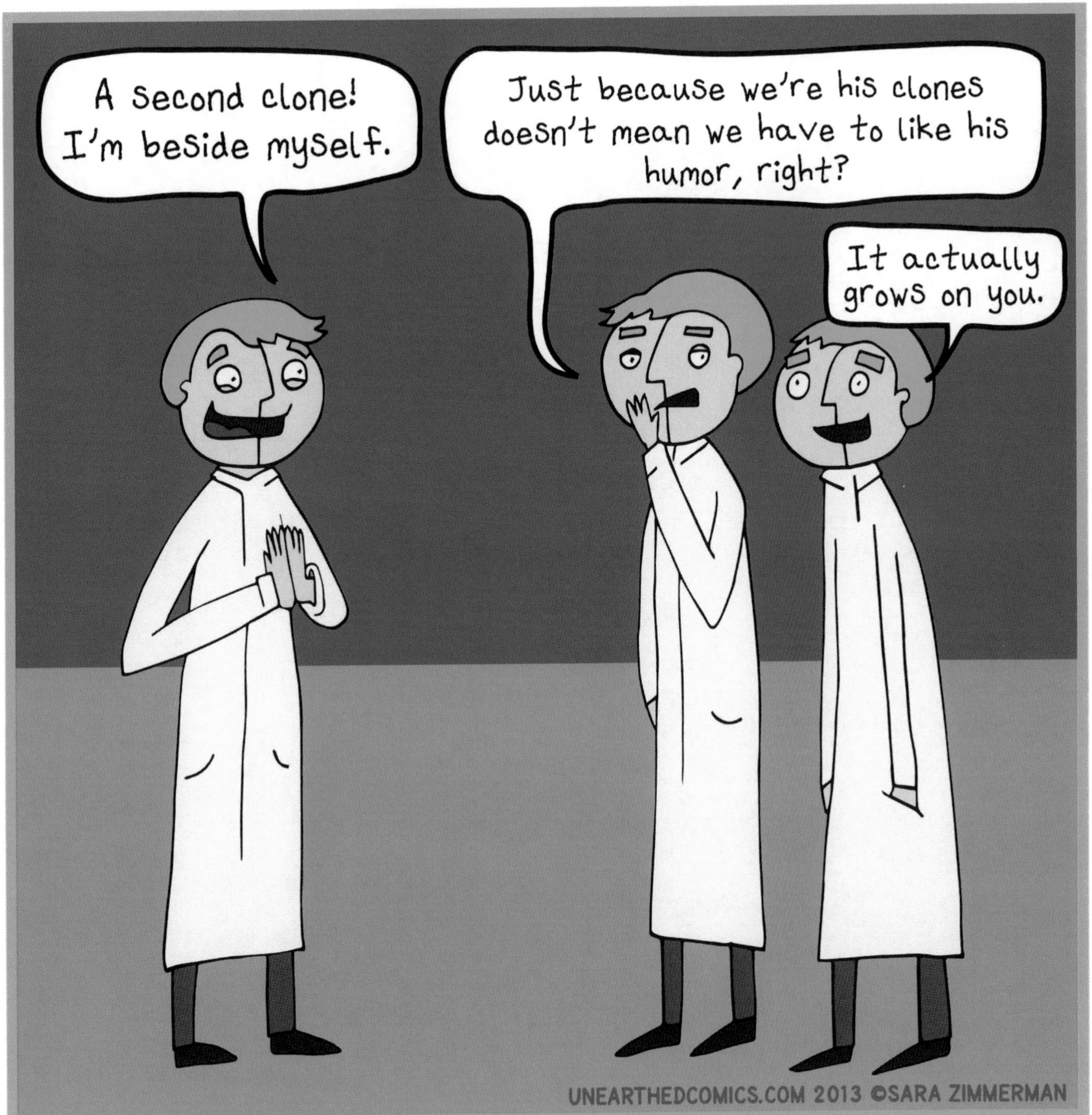
A second clone! I'm beside myself.
Just because we're his clones doesn't mean we have to like his humor, right?
It actually grows on you.
UNEARTHEDCOMICS.COM 2013 ©SARA ZIMMERMAN

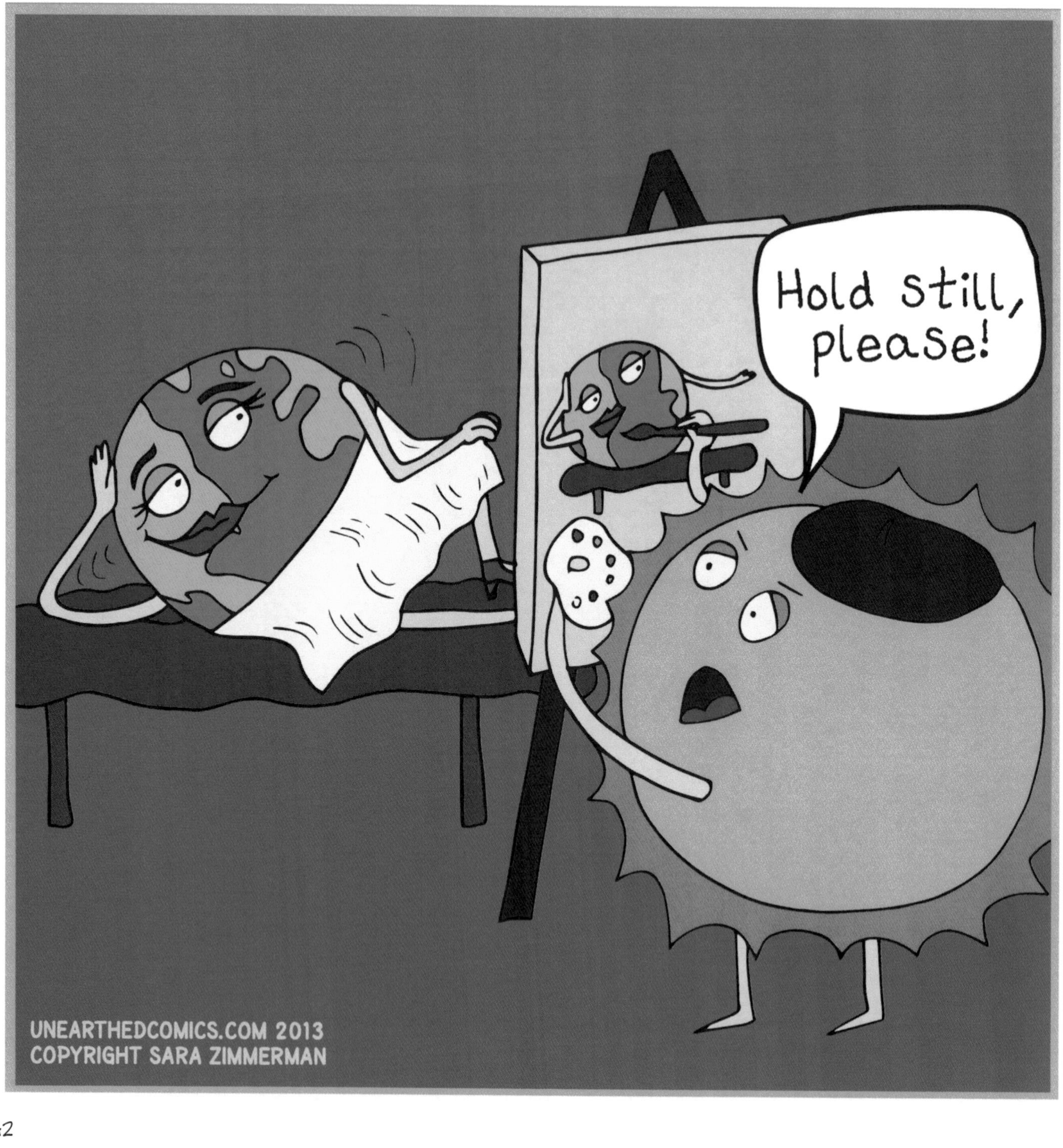
Hold still, please!
UNEARTHEDCOMICS.COM 2013
COPYRIGHT SARA ZIMMERMAN

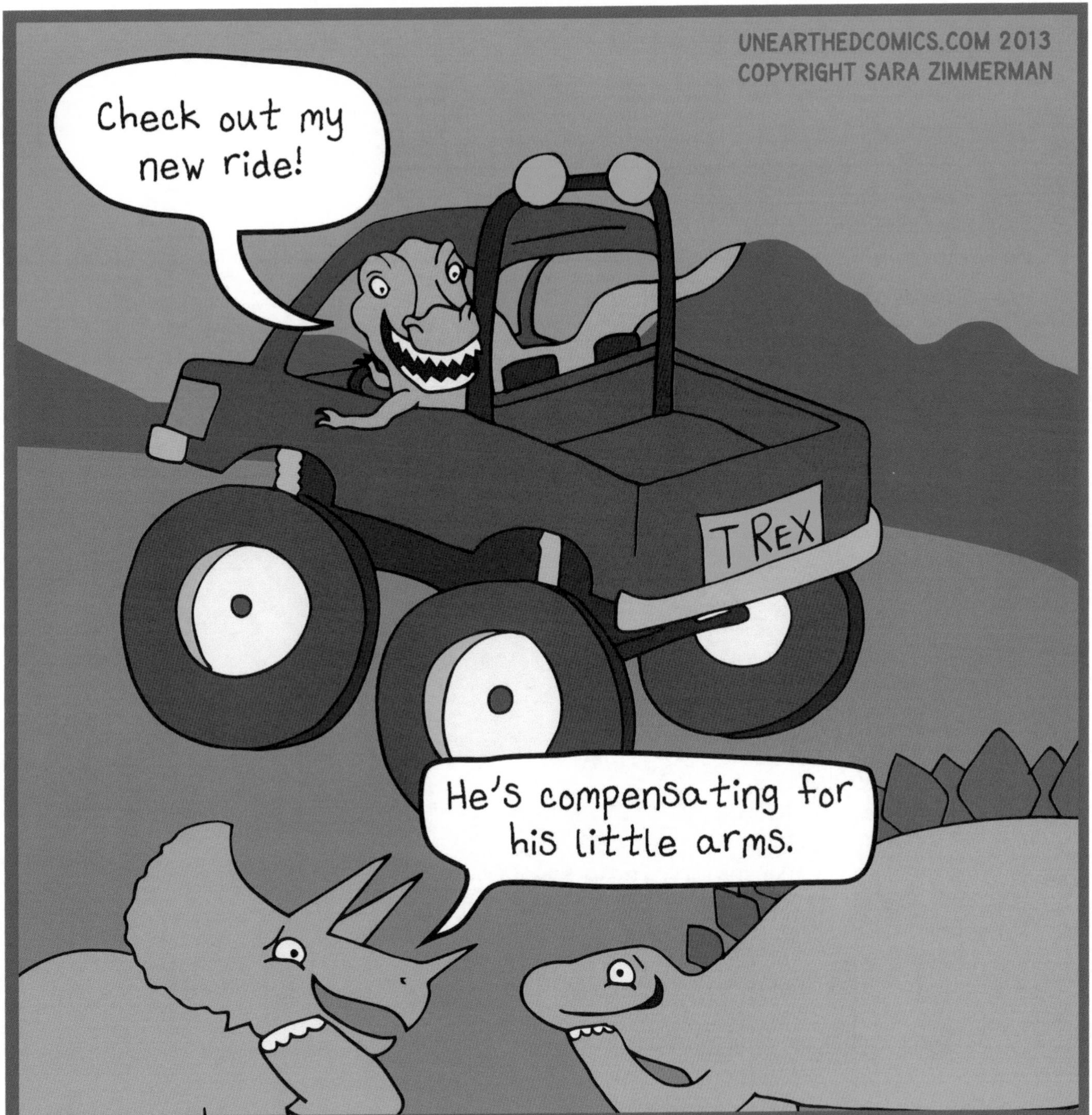
UNEARTHEDCOMICS.COM 2013
COPYRIGHT SARA ZIMMERMAN
Check out my new ride!
T REX
He's compensating for his little arms.

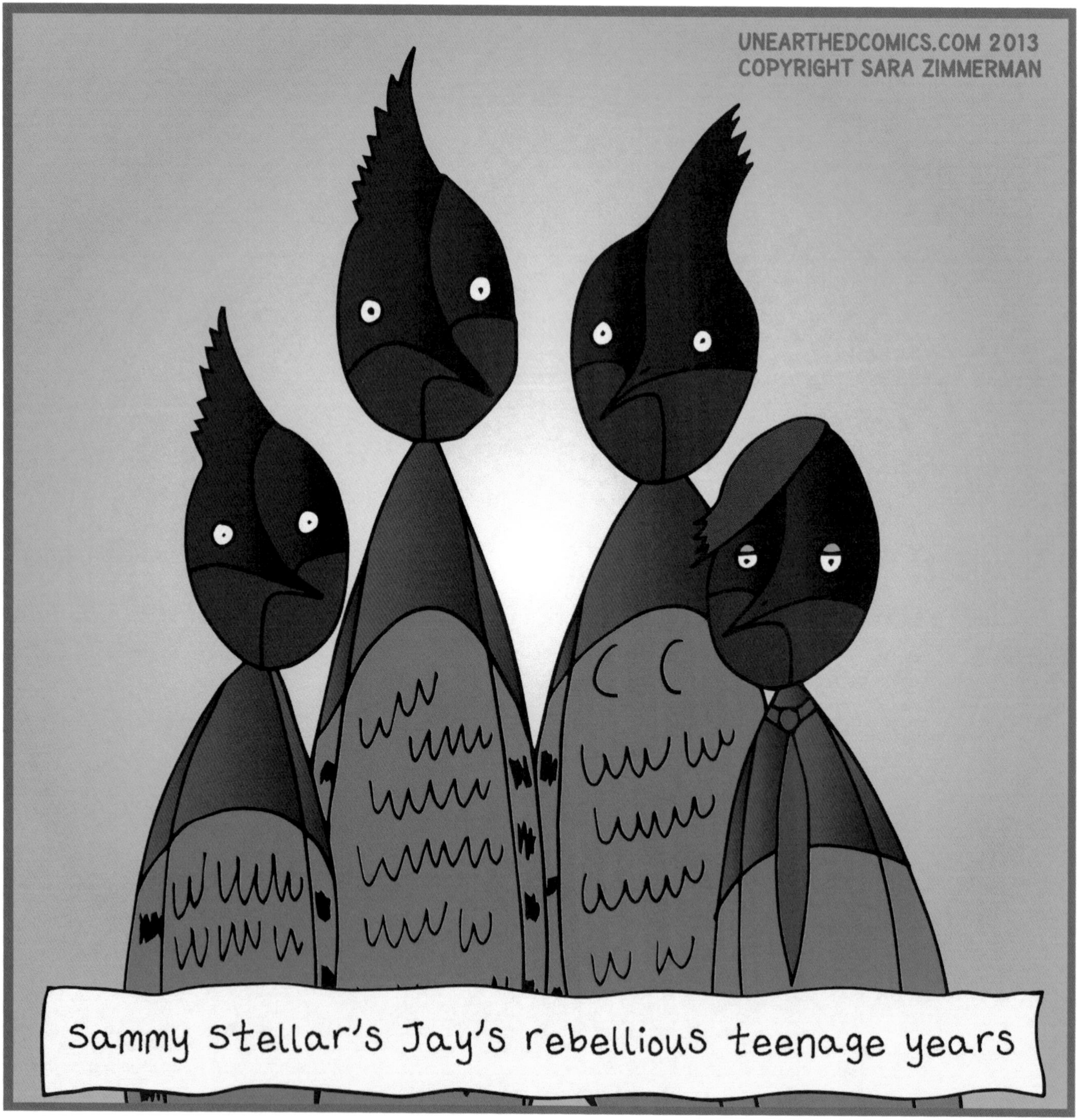
UNEARTHEDCOMICS.COM 2013
COPYRIGHT SARA ZIMMERMAN
Sammy Stellar's Jay's rebellious teenage years

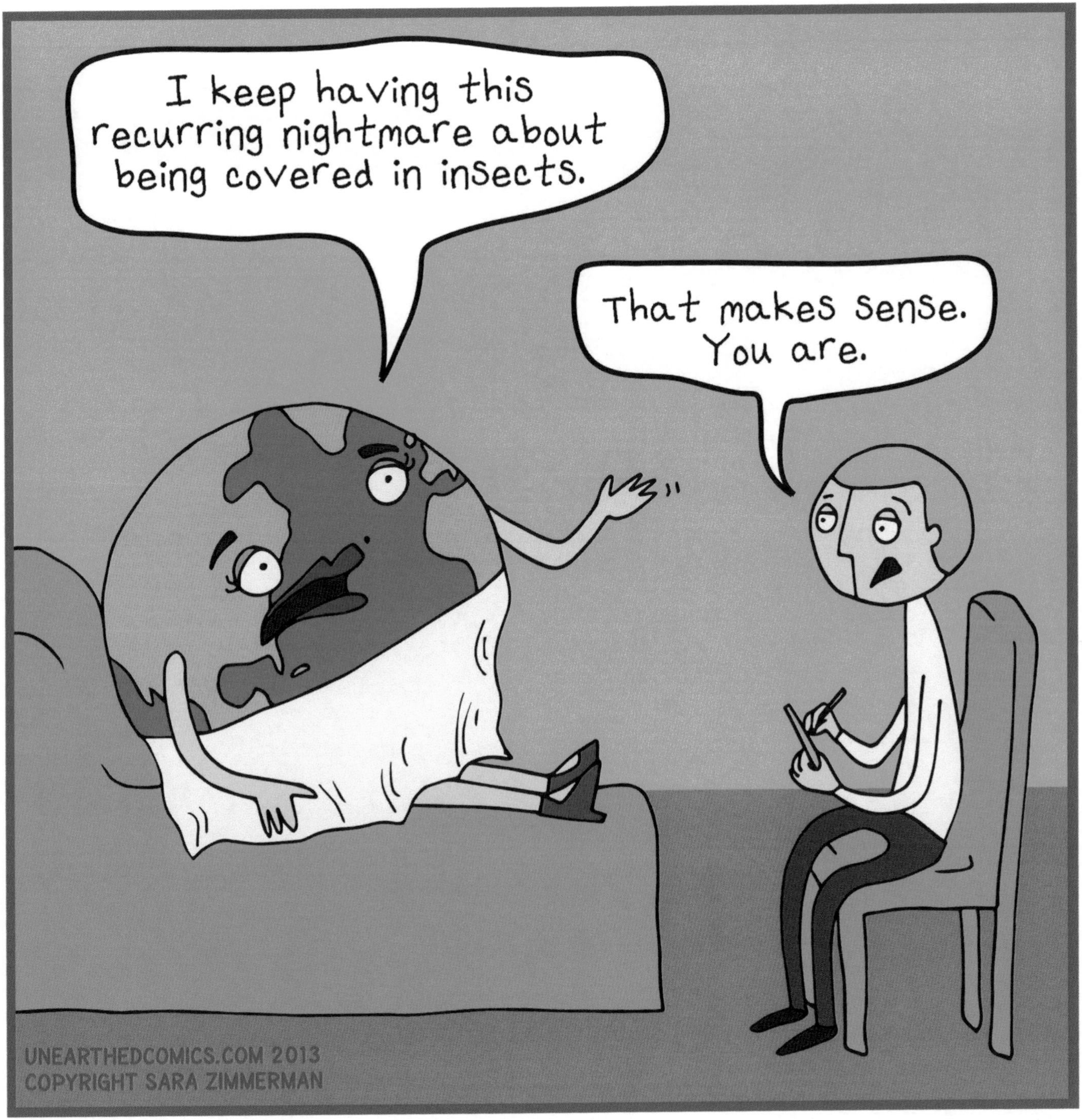
I keep having this recurring nightmare about being covered in insects.
That makes sense. You are.
UNEARTHEDCOMICS.COM 2013
COPYRIGHT SARA ZIMMERMAN

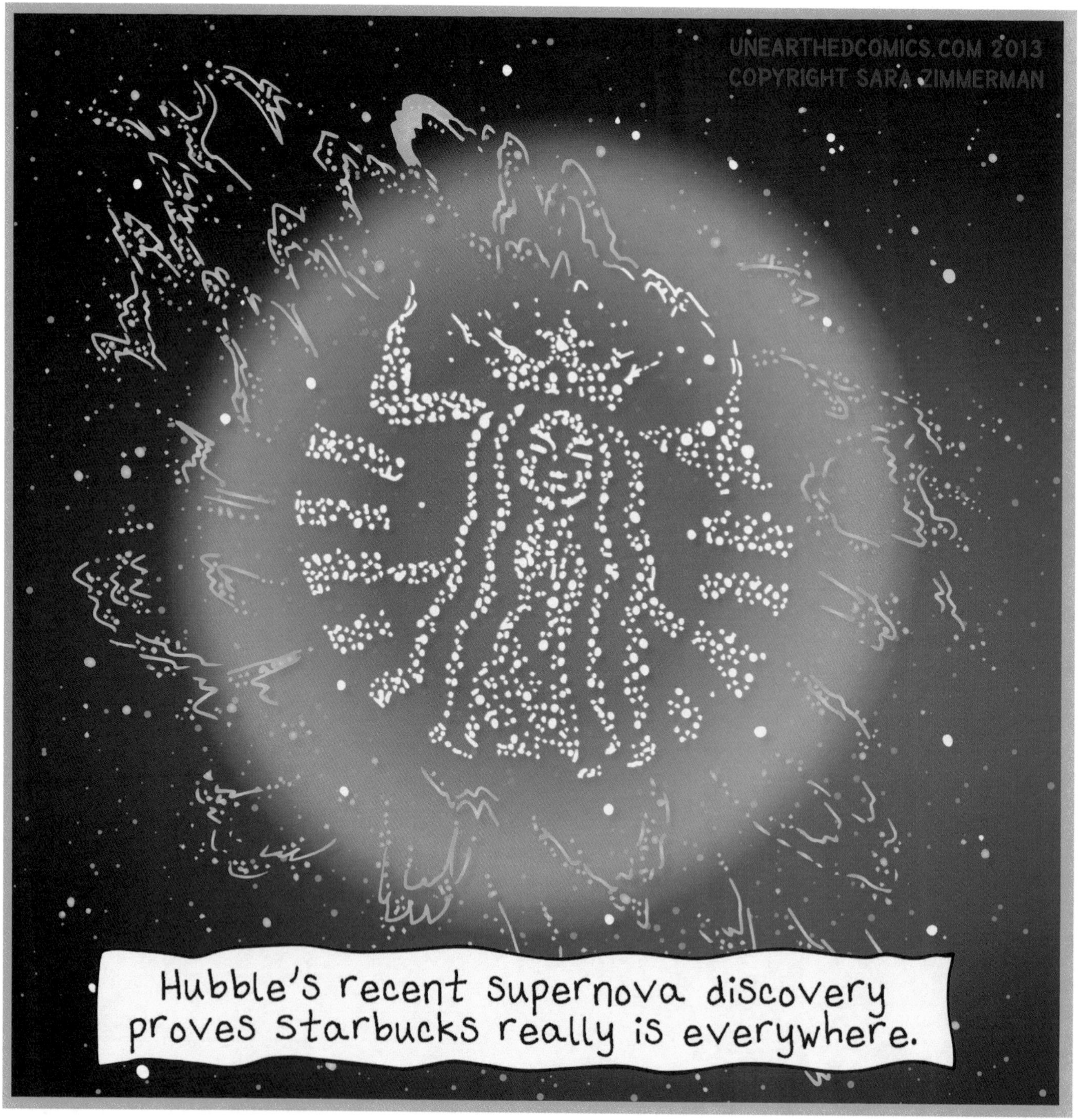
UNEARTHEDCOMICS.COM 2013
COPYRIGHT SARA ZIMMERMAN
Hubble's recent supernova discovery proves Starbucks really is everywhere.

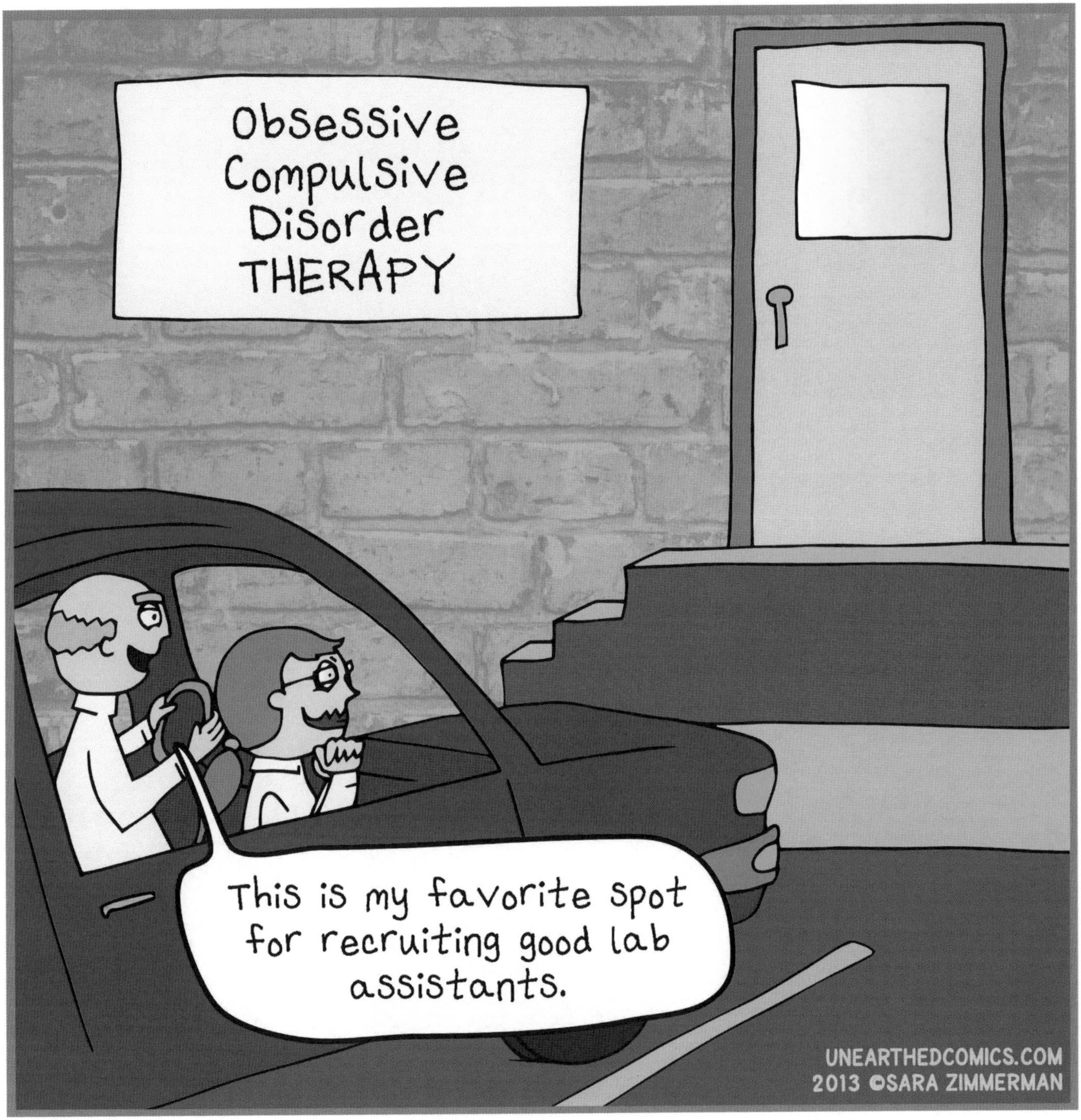

Obsessive Compulsive Disorder THERAPY
This is my favorite spot for recruiting good lab assistants.
UNEARTHEDCOMICS.COM
2013 ©SARA ZIMMERMAN

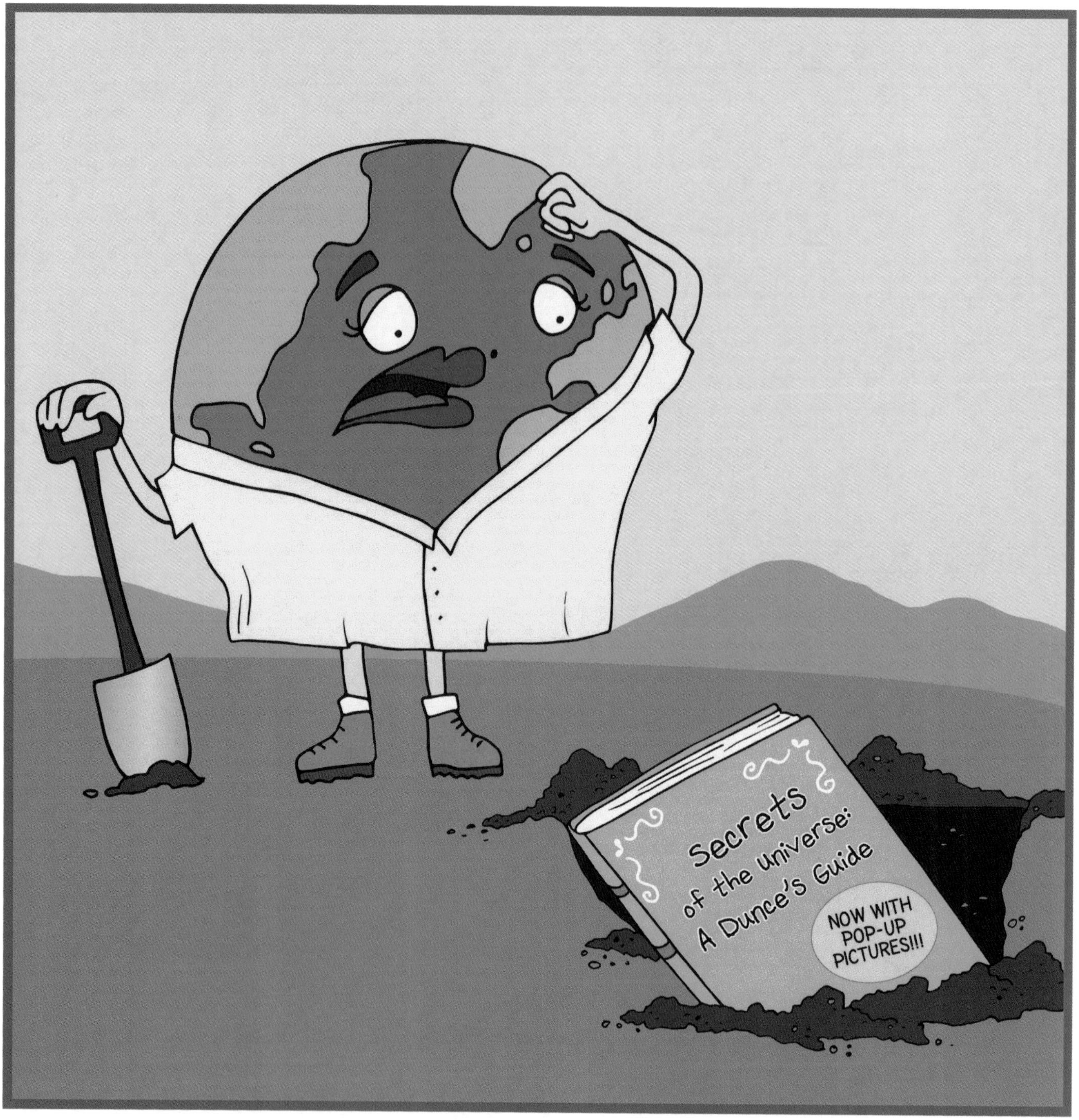
Secrets
of the Universe:
A Dunce's Guide
NOW WITH
POP-UP
PICTURES!!!

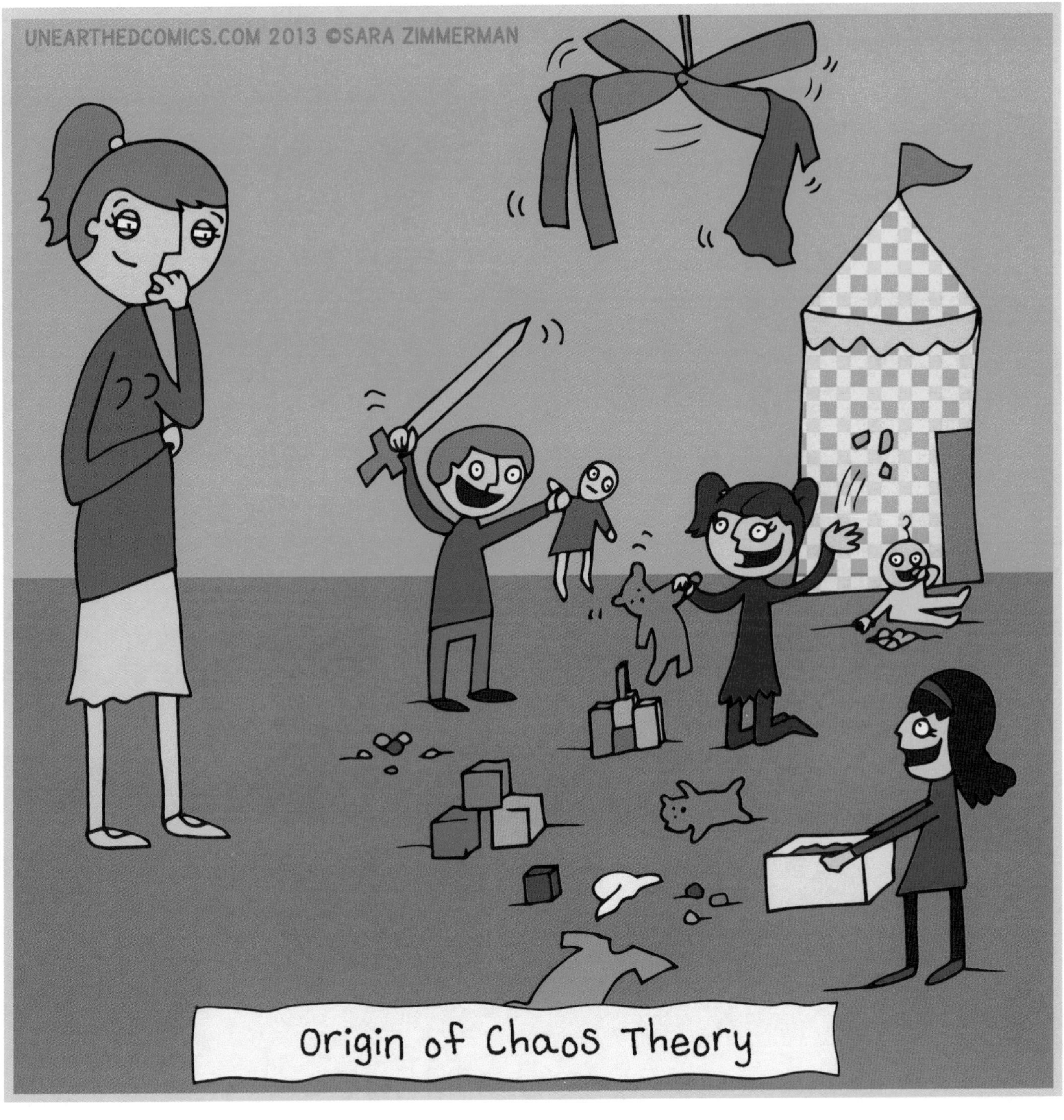
UNEARTHEDCOMICS.COM 2013 ©SARA ZIMMERMAN
Origin of Chaos Theory

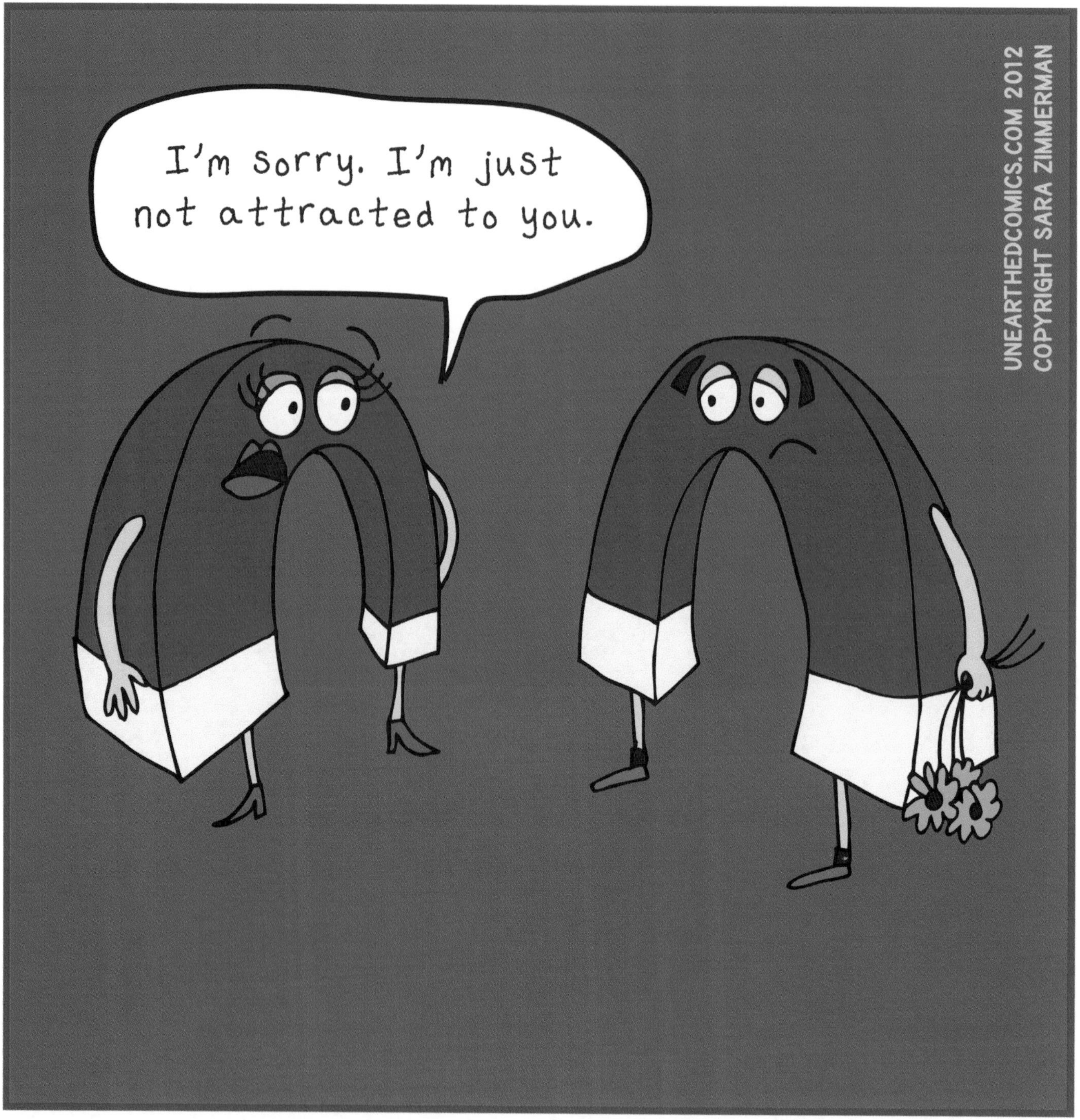
I'm sorry. I'm just not attracted to you.
UNEARTHEDCOMICS.COM 2012
COPYRIGHT SARA ZIMMERMAN

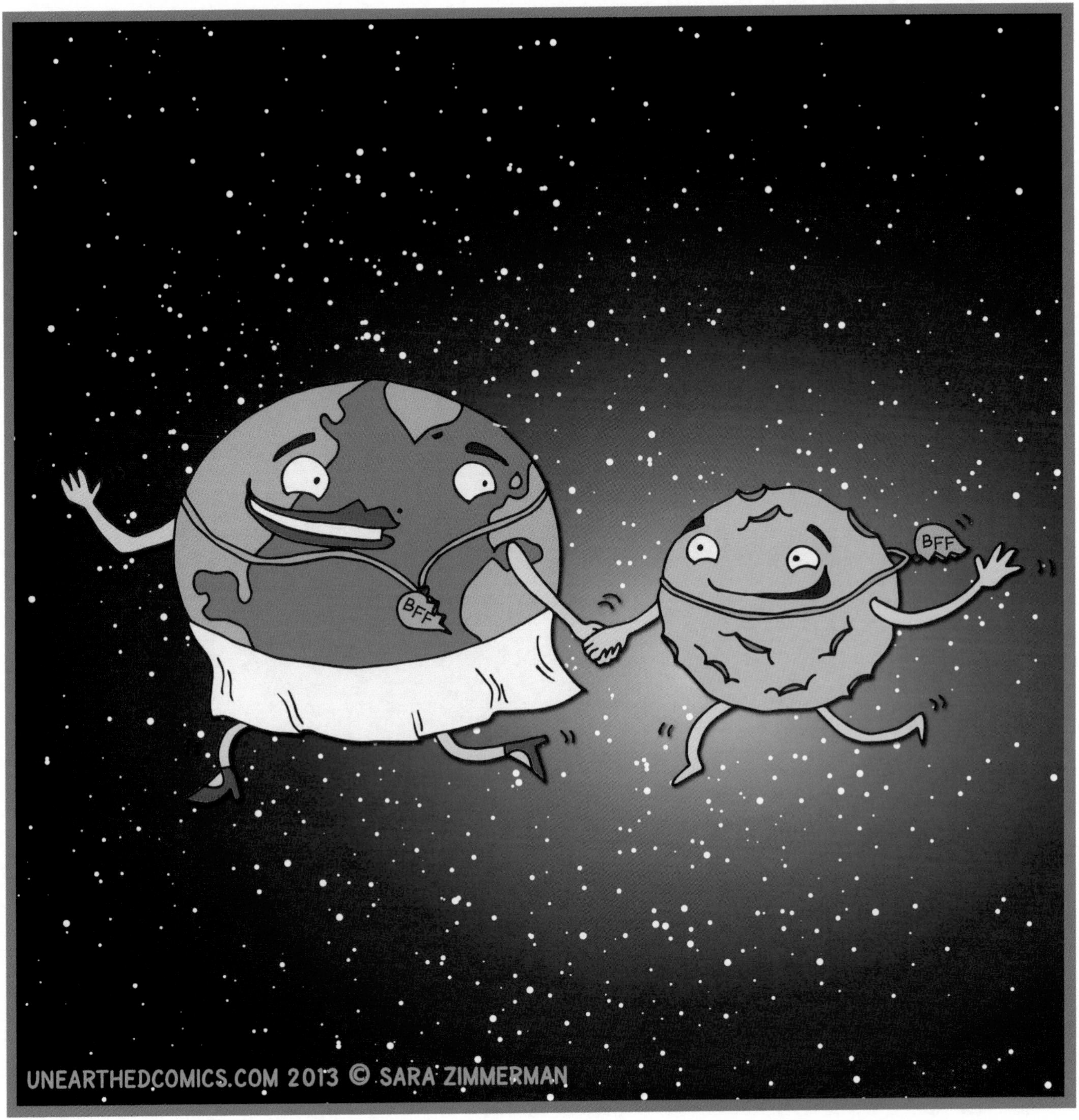
BFF
BFF
UNEARTHEDCOMICS.COM 2013 © SARA ZIMMERMAN

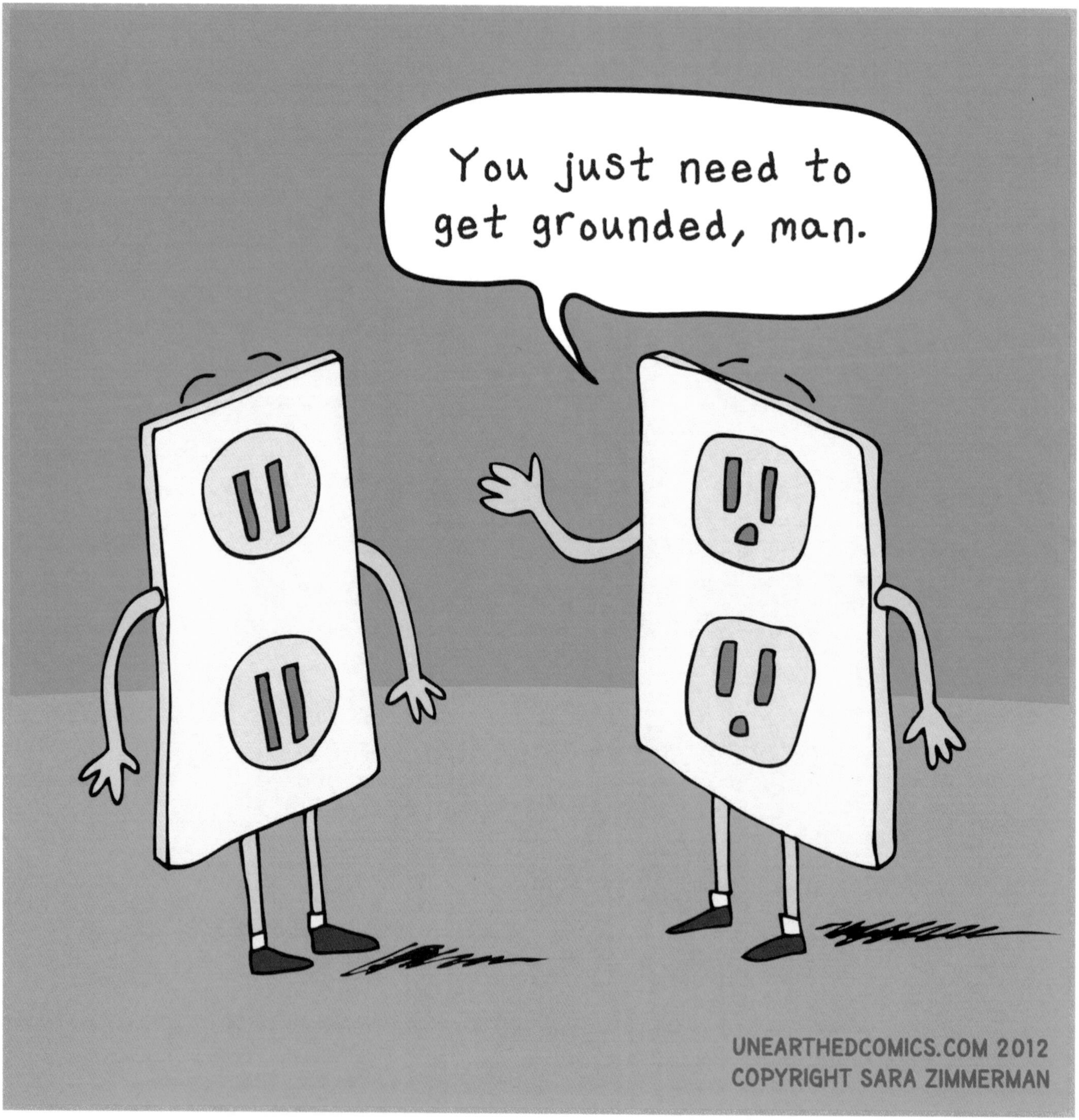
You just need to get grounded, man.
UNEARTHEDCOMICS.COM 2012
COPYRIGHT SARA ZIMMERMAN

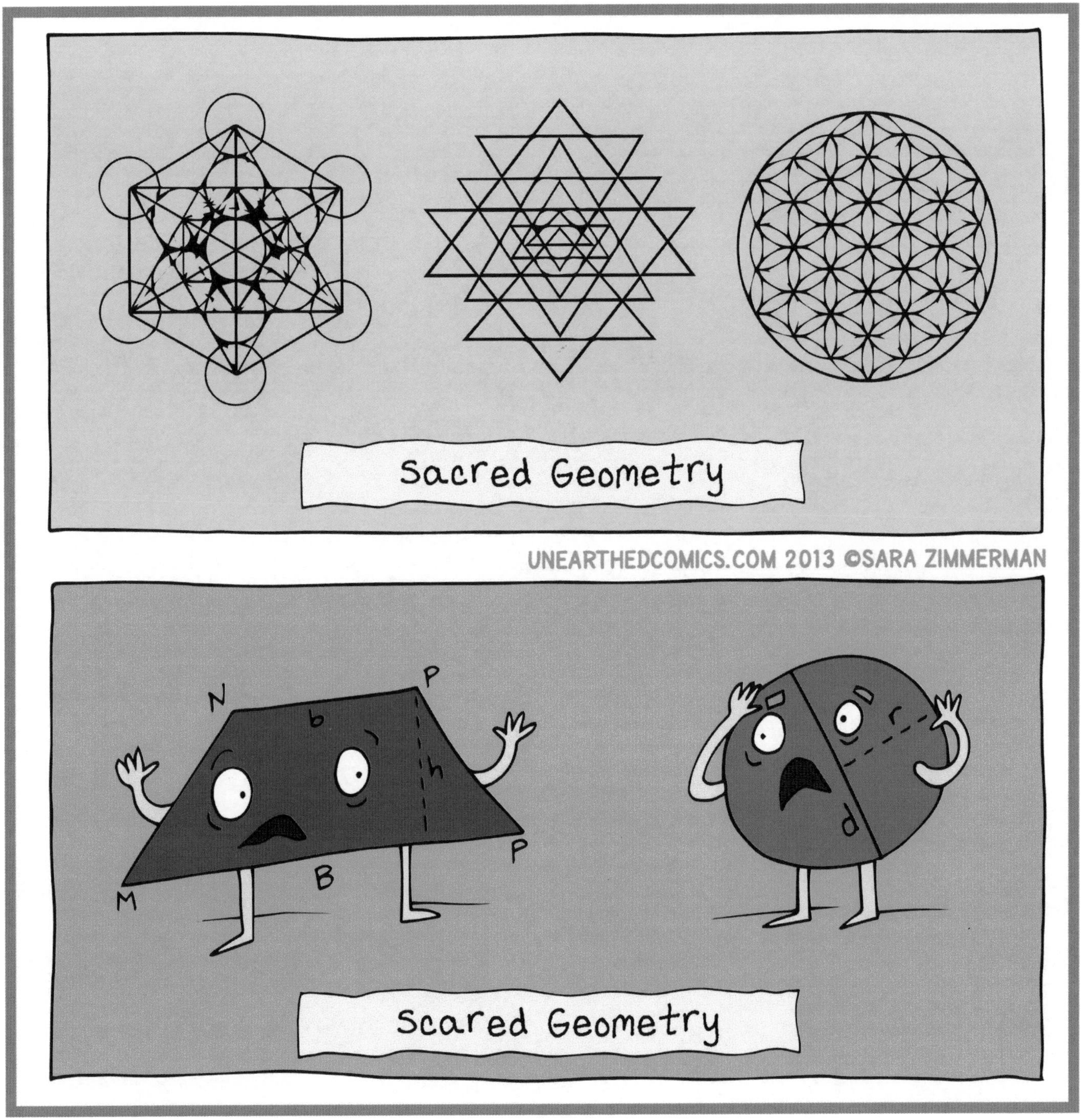

Sacred Geometry
UNEARTHEDCOMICS.COM 2013 ©SARA ZIMMERMAN
N
P
b
h
P
M
B
r
d
Scared Geometry

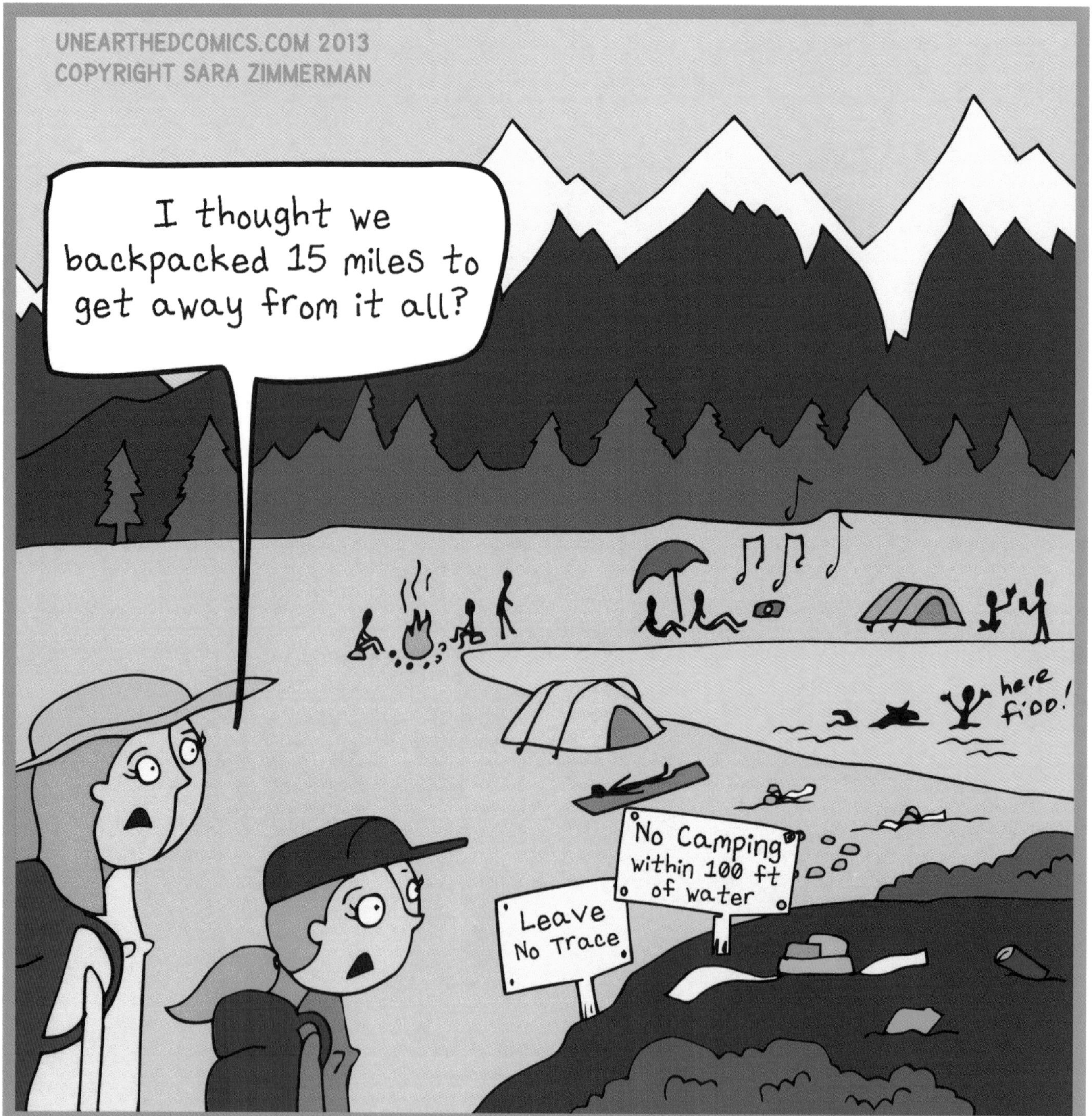
UNEARTHEDCOMICS.COM 2013
COPYRIGHT SARA ZIMMERMAN
I thought we backpacked 15 miles to get away from it all?
here fido!
No Camping within 100 ft of water
Leave No Trace

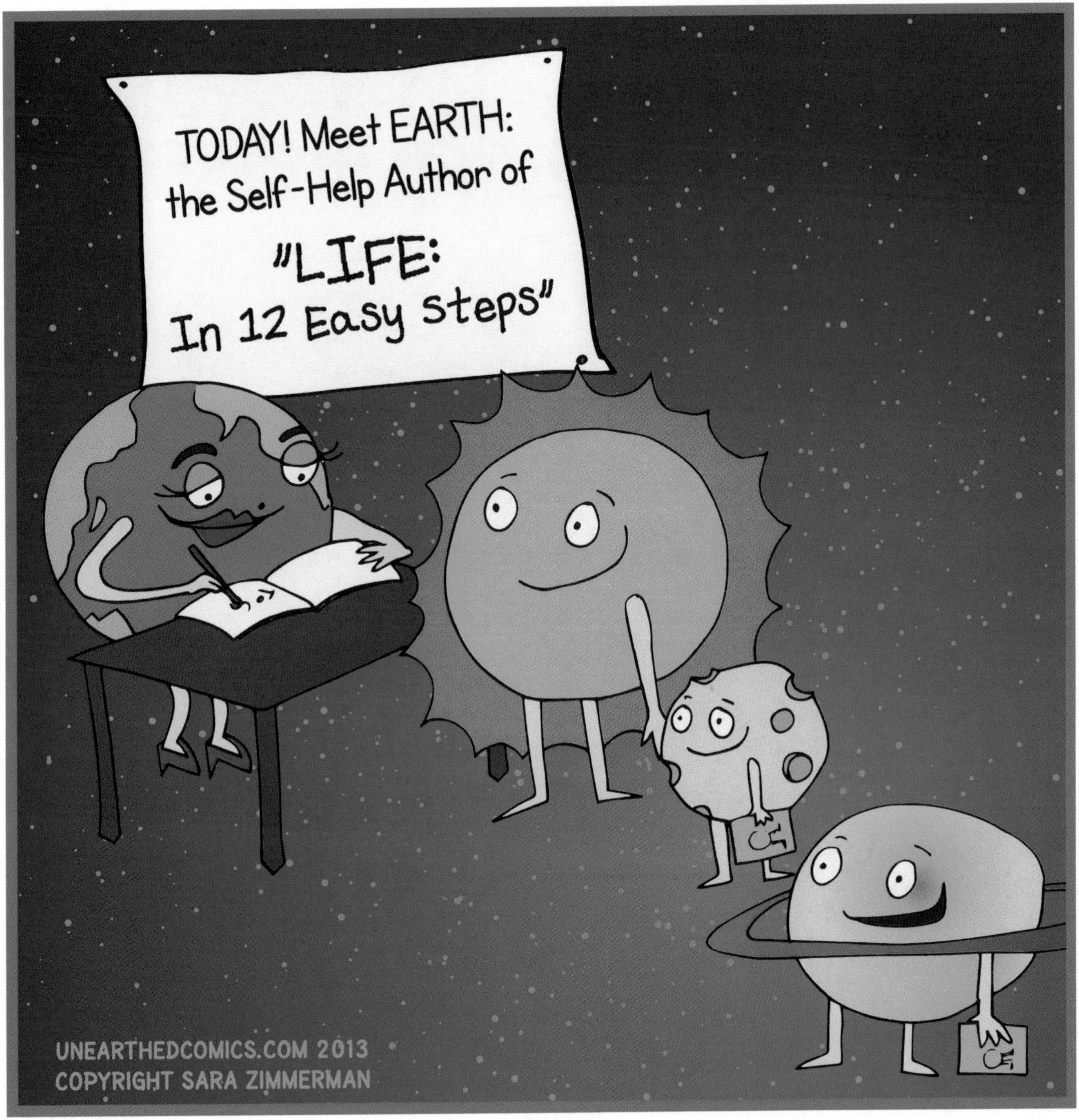
TODAY! Meet EARTH:
the Self-Help Author of
"LIFE:
In 12 Easy Steps"
UNEARTHEDCOMICS.COM 2013
COPYRIGHT SARA ZIMMERMAN

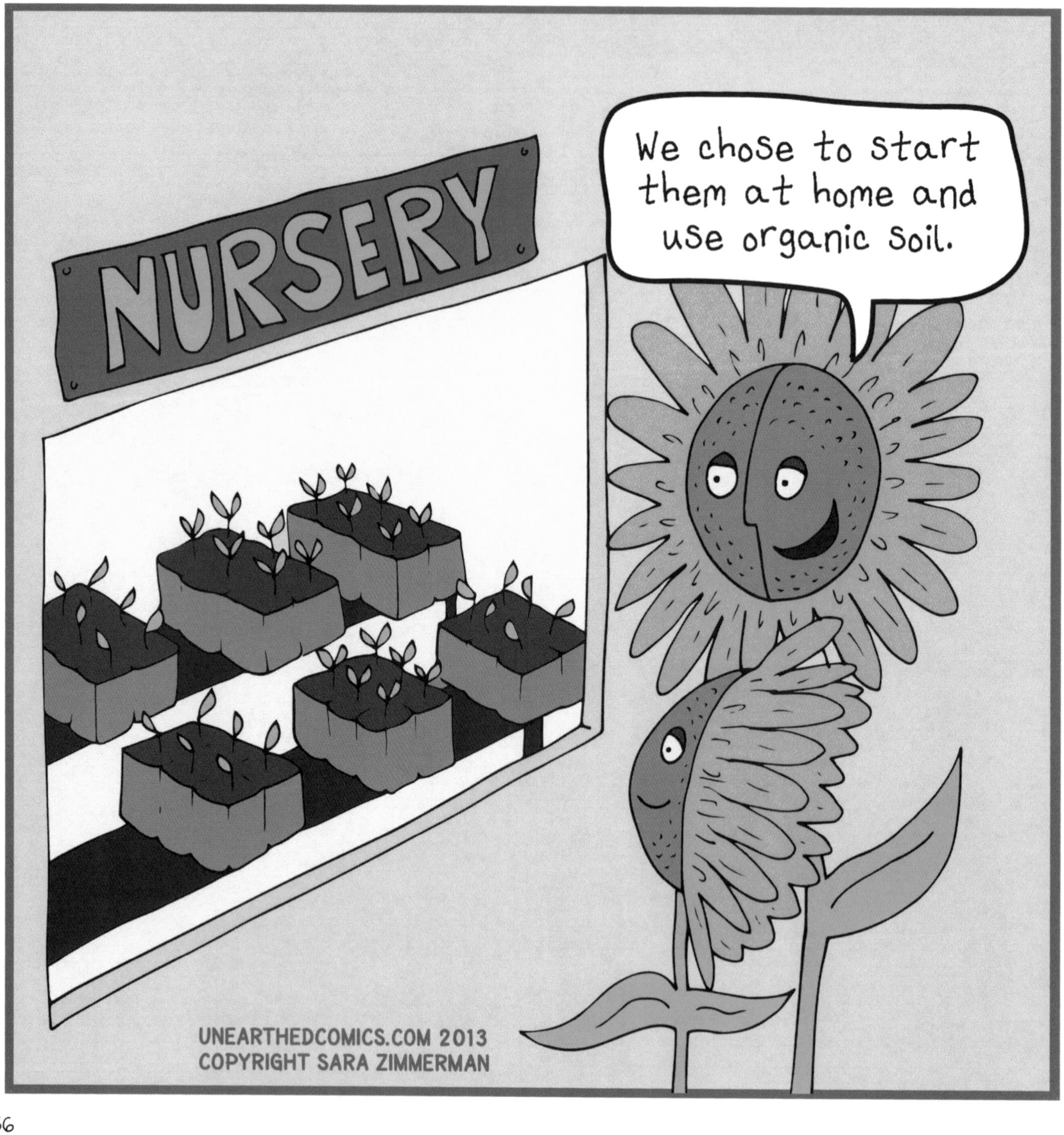
NURSERY
We chose to start them at home and use organic soil.
UNEARTHEDCOMICS.COM 2013
COPYRIGHT SARA ZIMMERMAN

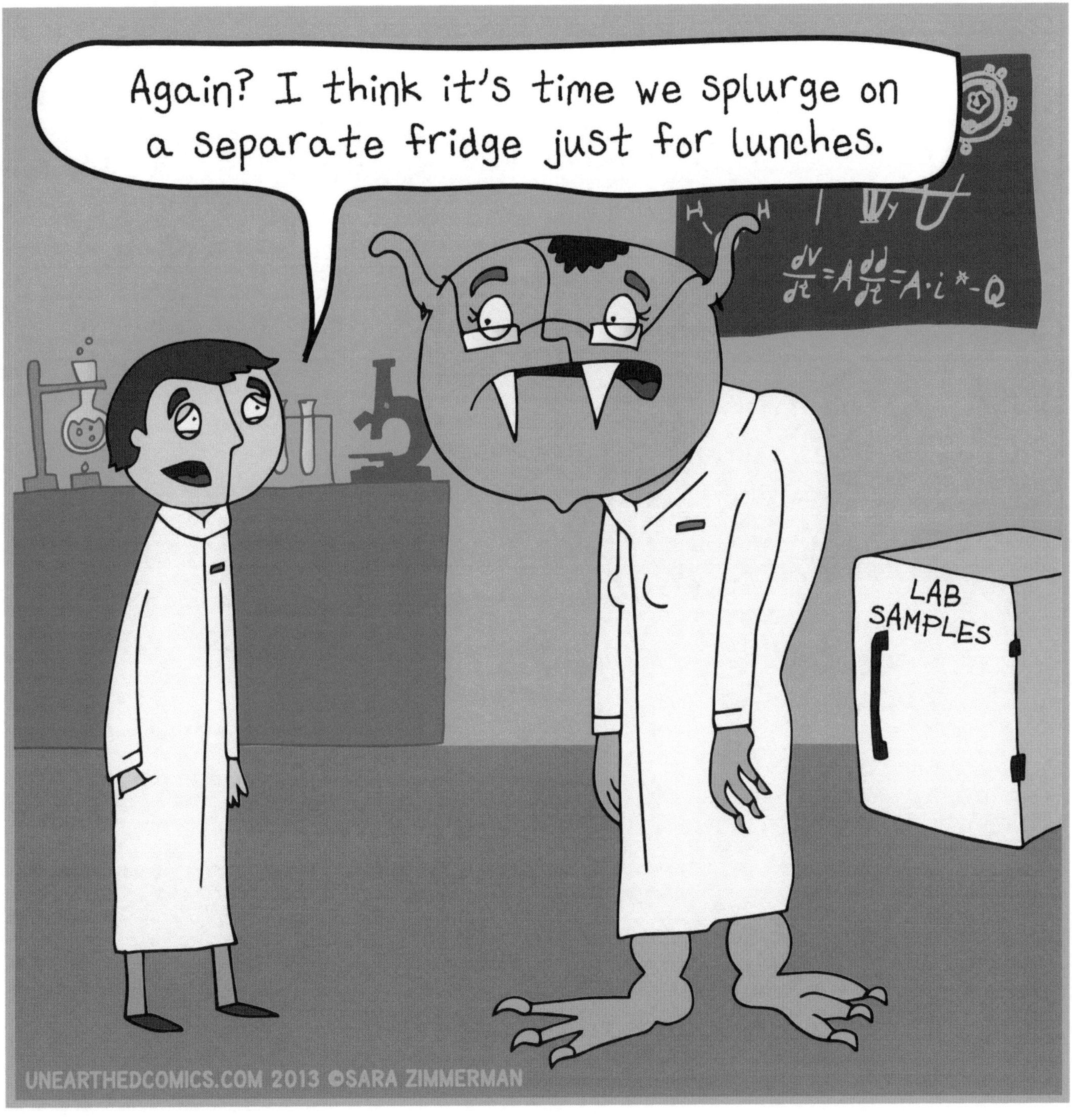
Again? I think it's time we splurge on a separate fridge just for lunches.
LAB SAMPLES
UNEARTHEDCOMICS.COM 2013 ©SARA ZIMMERMAN

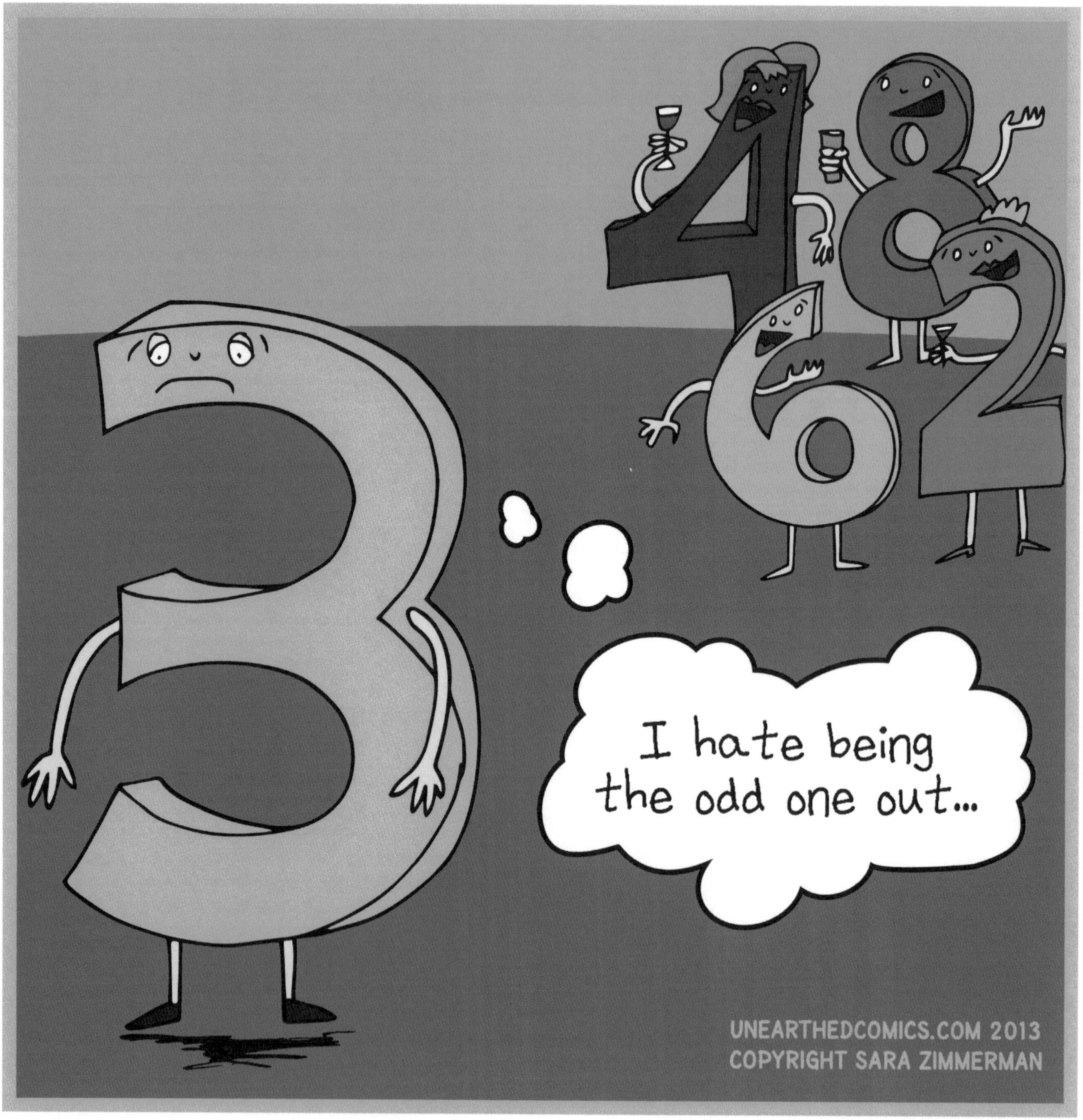
I hate being the odd one out...
UNEARTHEDCOMICS.COM 2013
COPYRIGHT SARA ZIMMERMAN

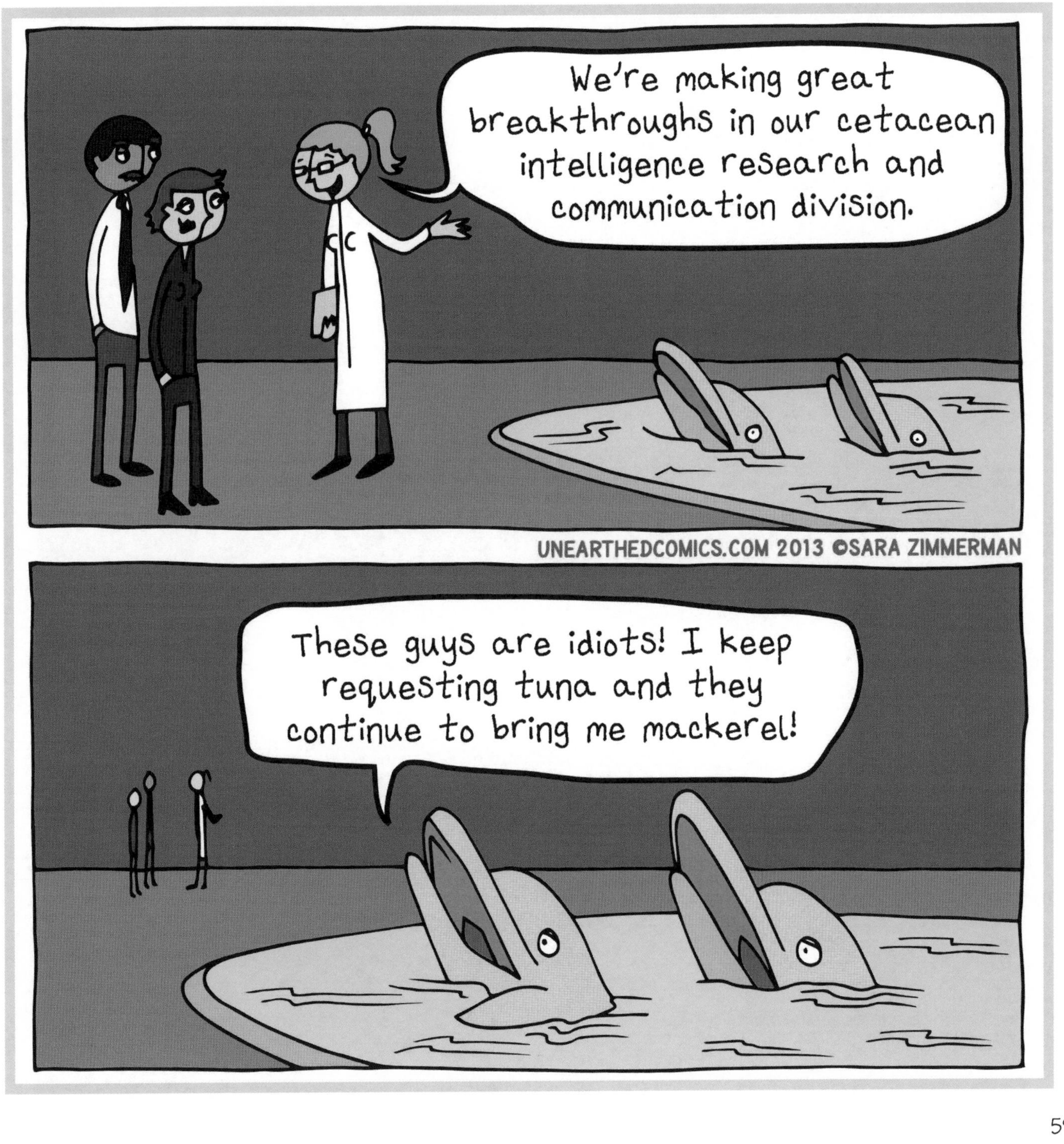
We're making great breakthroughs in our cetacean intelligence research and communication division.
UNEARTHEDCOMICS.COM 2013 ©SARA ZIMMERMAN
These guys are idiots! I keep requesting tuna and they continue to bring me mackerel!

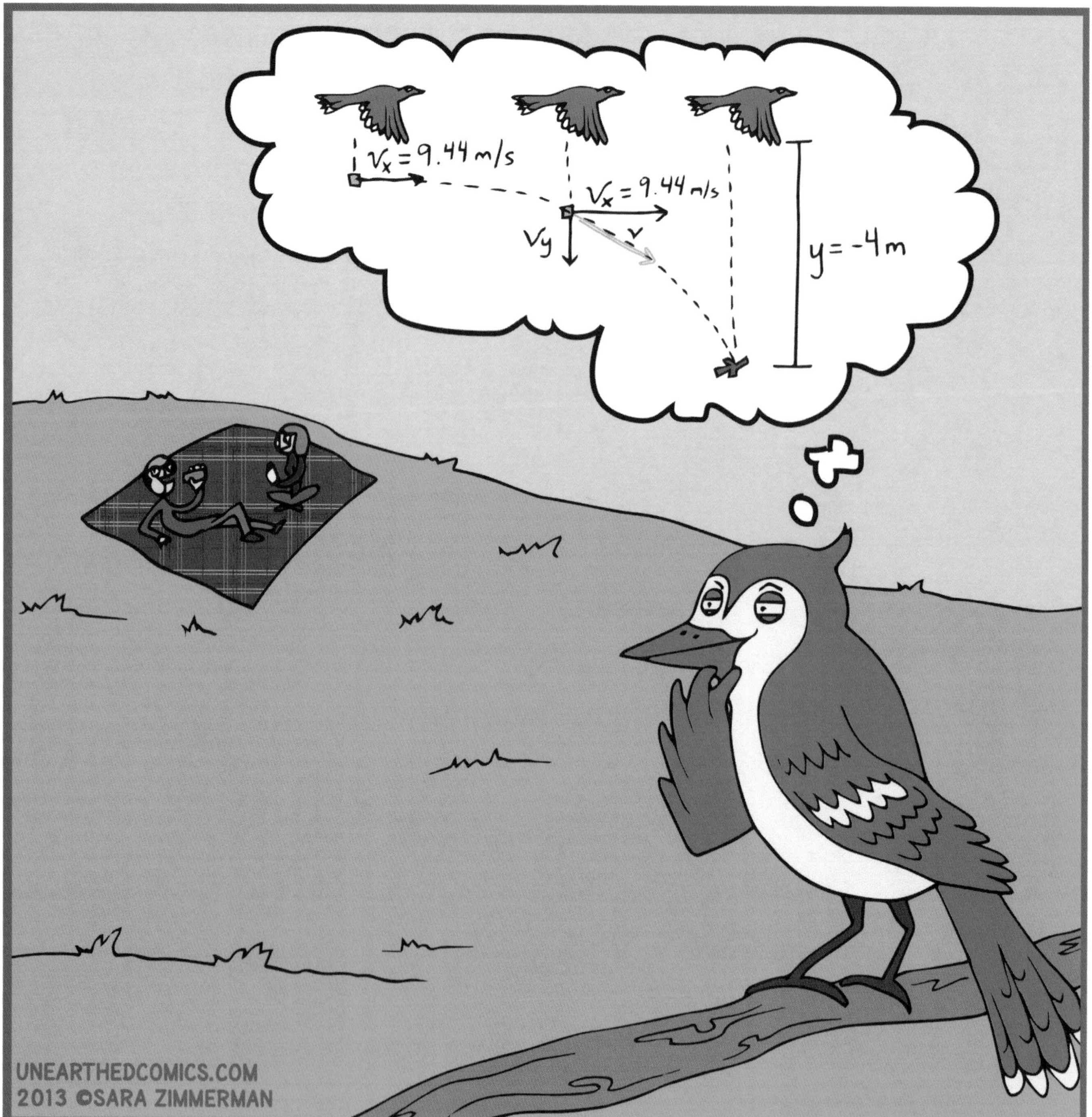

$v_x = 9.44$ m/s
$v_x = 9.44$ m/s
v_y
v
$y = -4$ m
UNEARTHEDCOMICS.COM
2013 ©SARA ZIMMERMAN

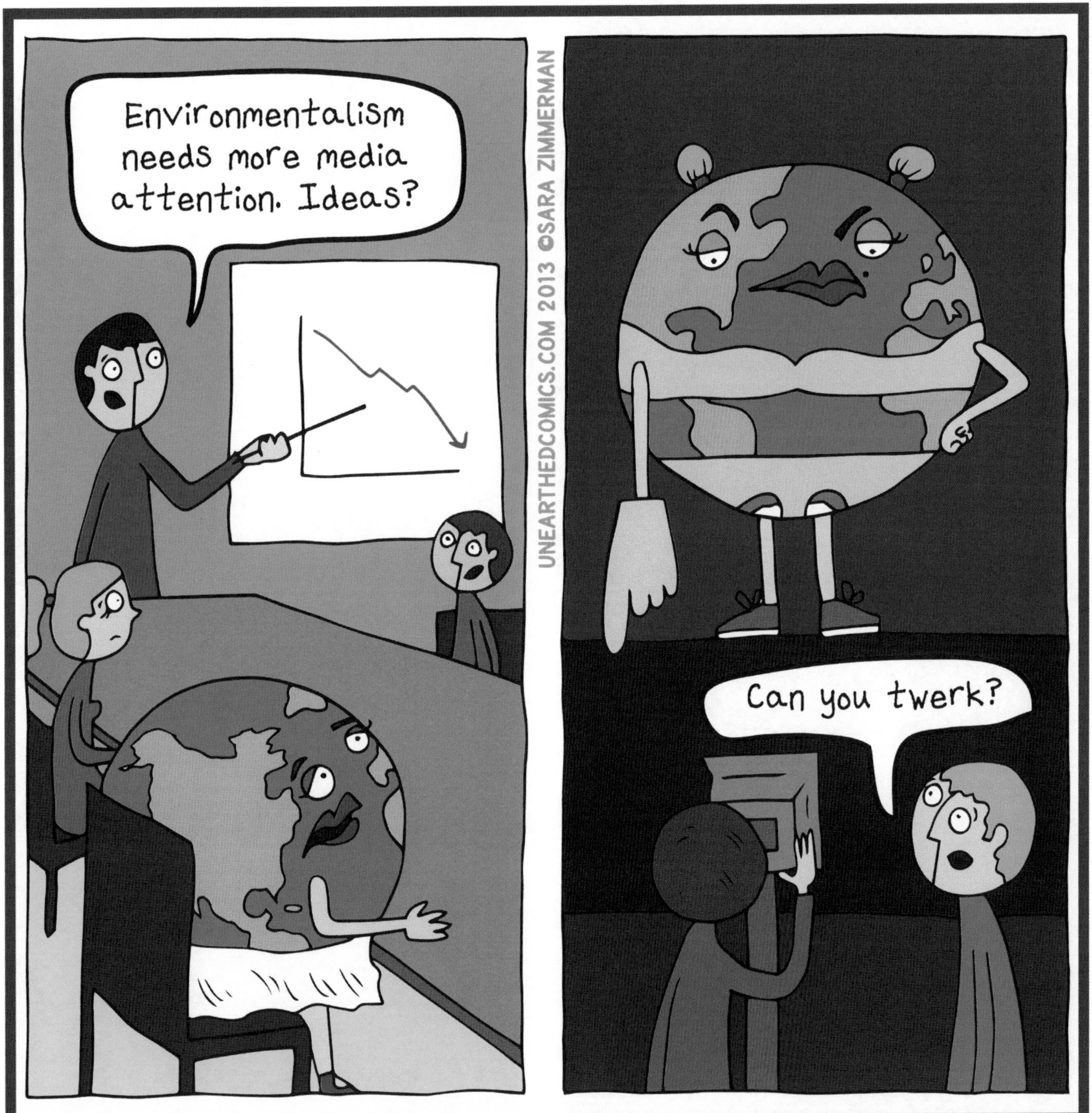
Environmentalism needs more media attention. Ideas?
UNEARTHEDCOMICS.COM 2013 ©SARA ZIMMERMAN
Can you twerk?

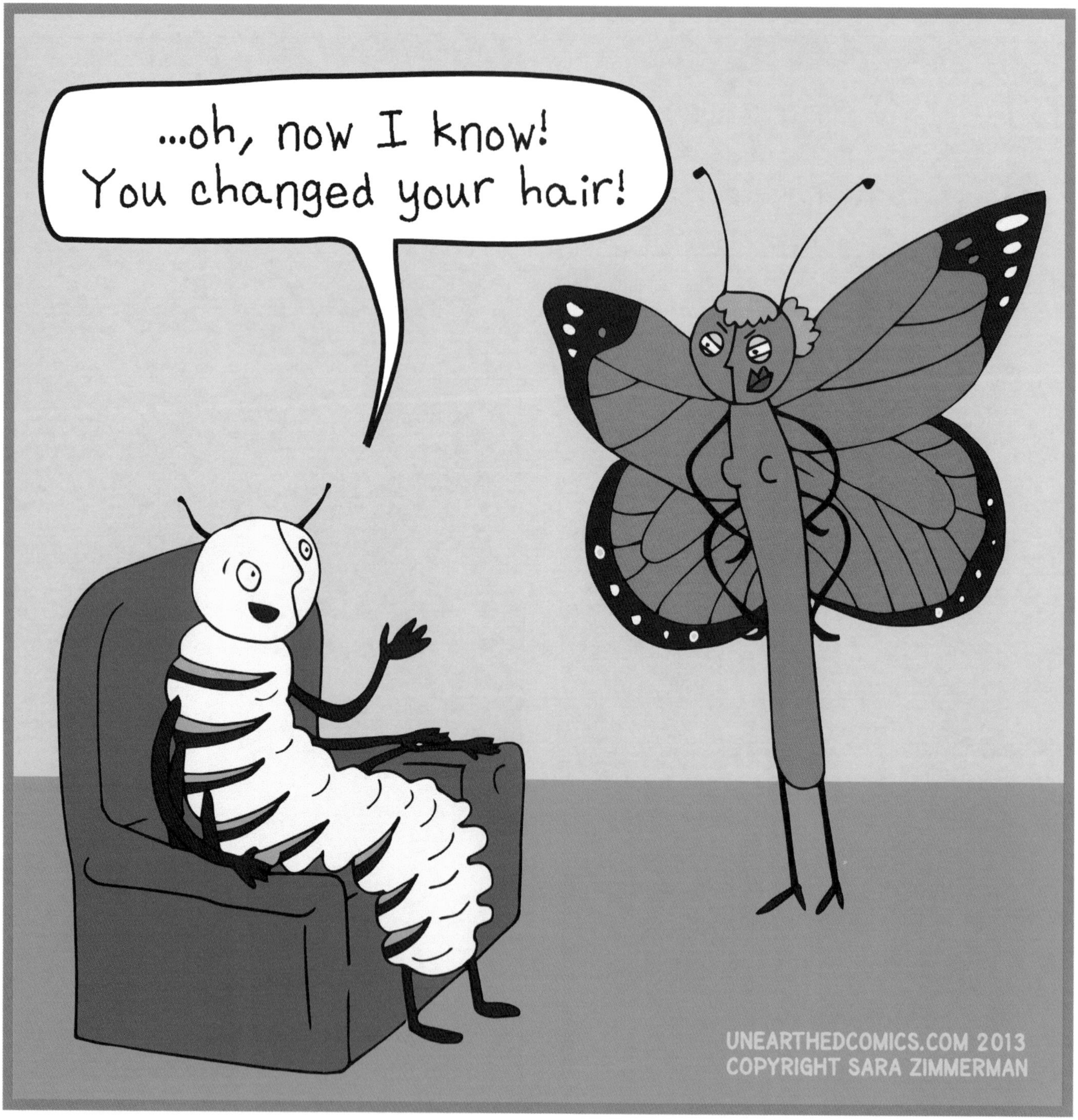
...oh, now I know! You changed your hair!
UNEARTHEDCOMICS.COM 2013
COPYRIGHT SARA ZIMMERMAN

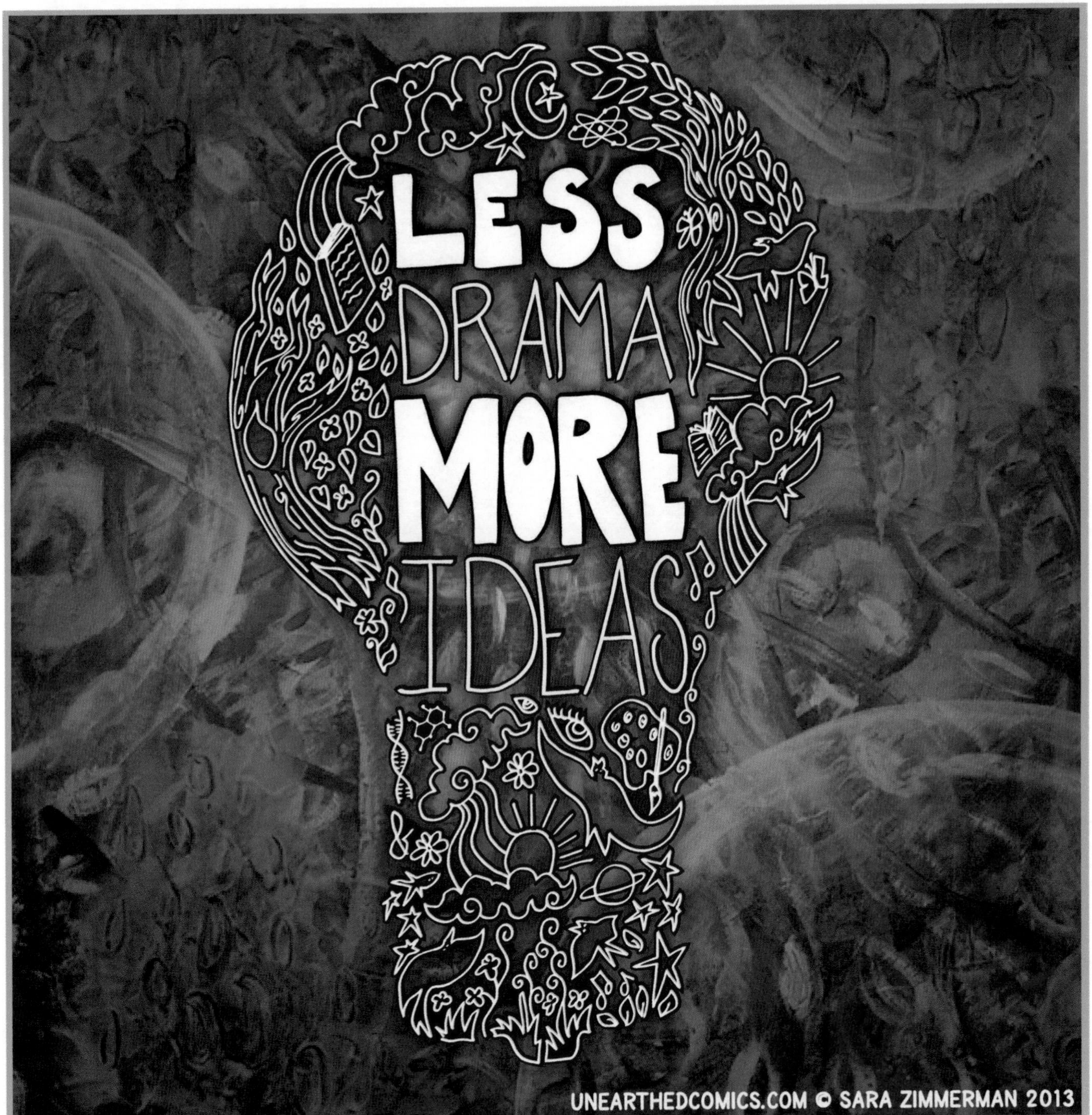
LESS
DRAMA
MORE
IDEAS
UNEARTHEDCOMICS.COM © SARA ZIMMERMAN 2013

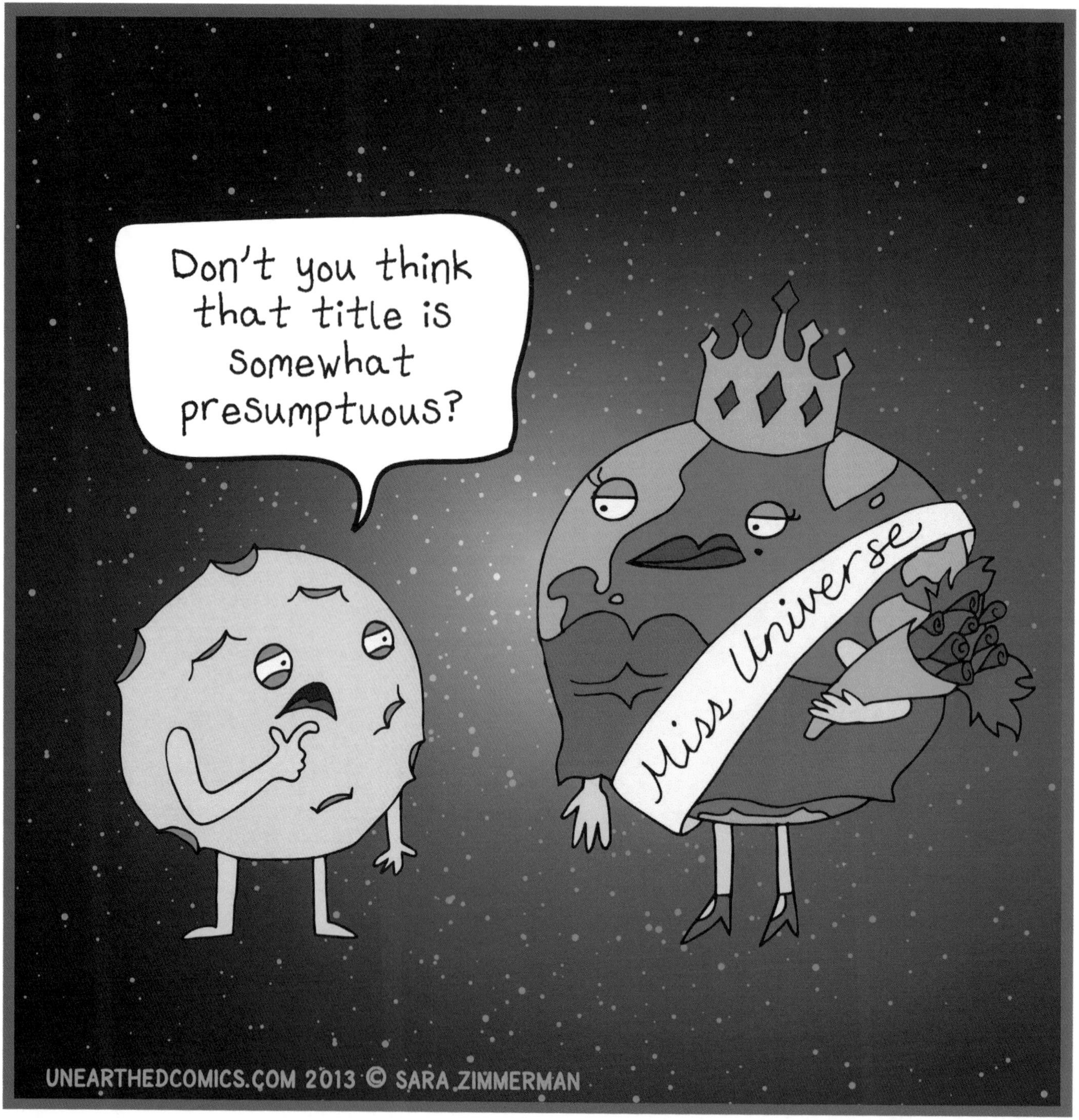
Don't you think that title is somewhat presumptuous?
Miss Universe
UNEARTHEDCOMICS.COM 2013 © SARA ZIMMERMAN

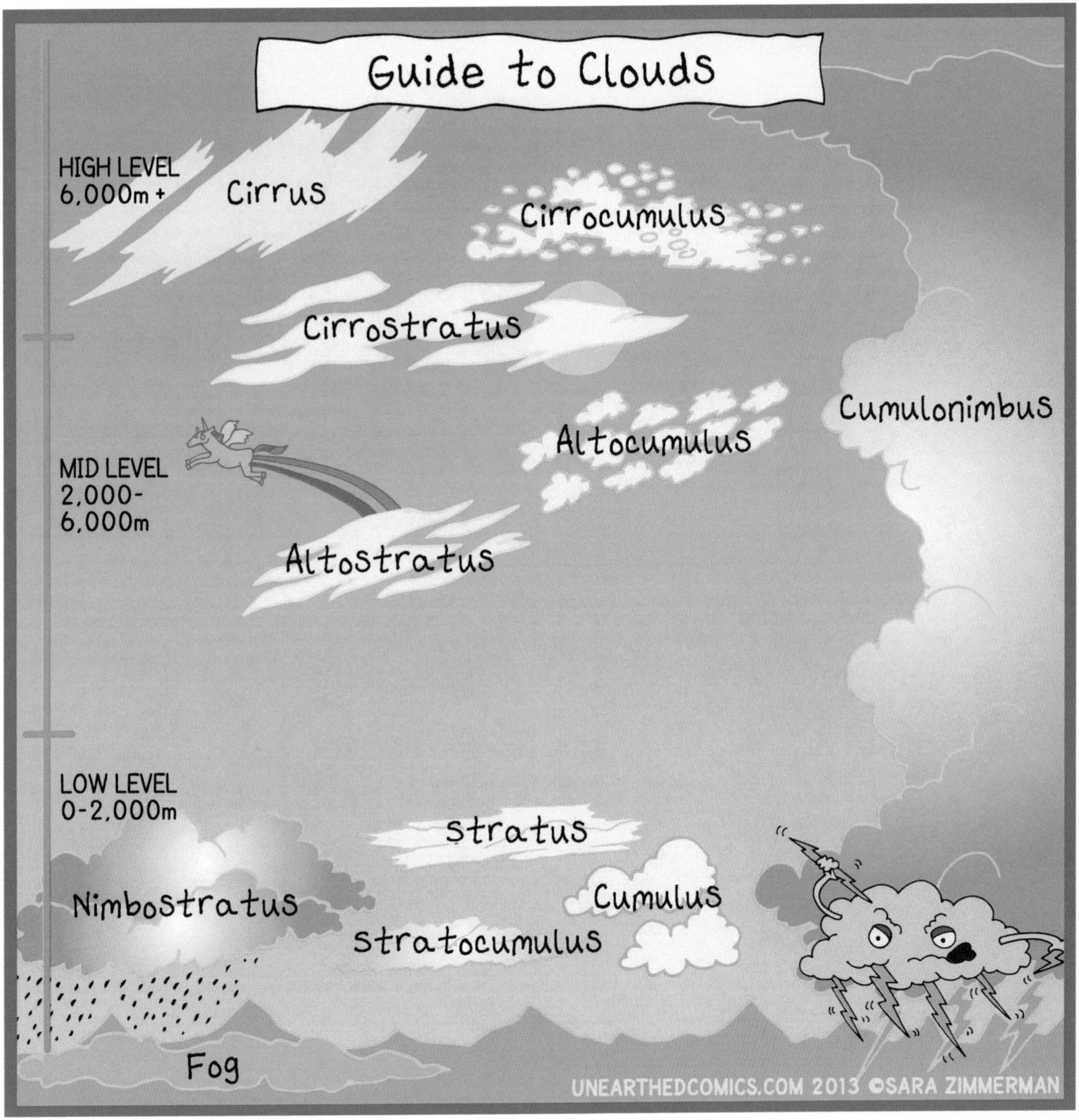
Guide to Clouds
HIGH LEVEL
6,000m +
Cirrus
Cirrocumulus
Cirrostratus
Cumulonimbus
Altocumulus
MID LEVEL
2,000-
6,000m
Altostratus
LOW LEVEL
0-2,000m
Stratus
Nimbostratus
Cumulus
Stratocumulus
Fog
UNEARTHEDCOMICS.COM 2013 ©SARA ZIMMERMAN

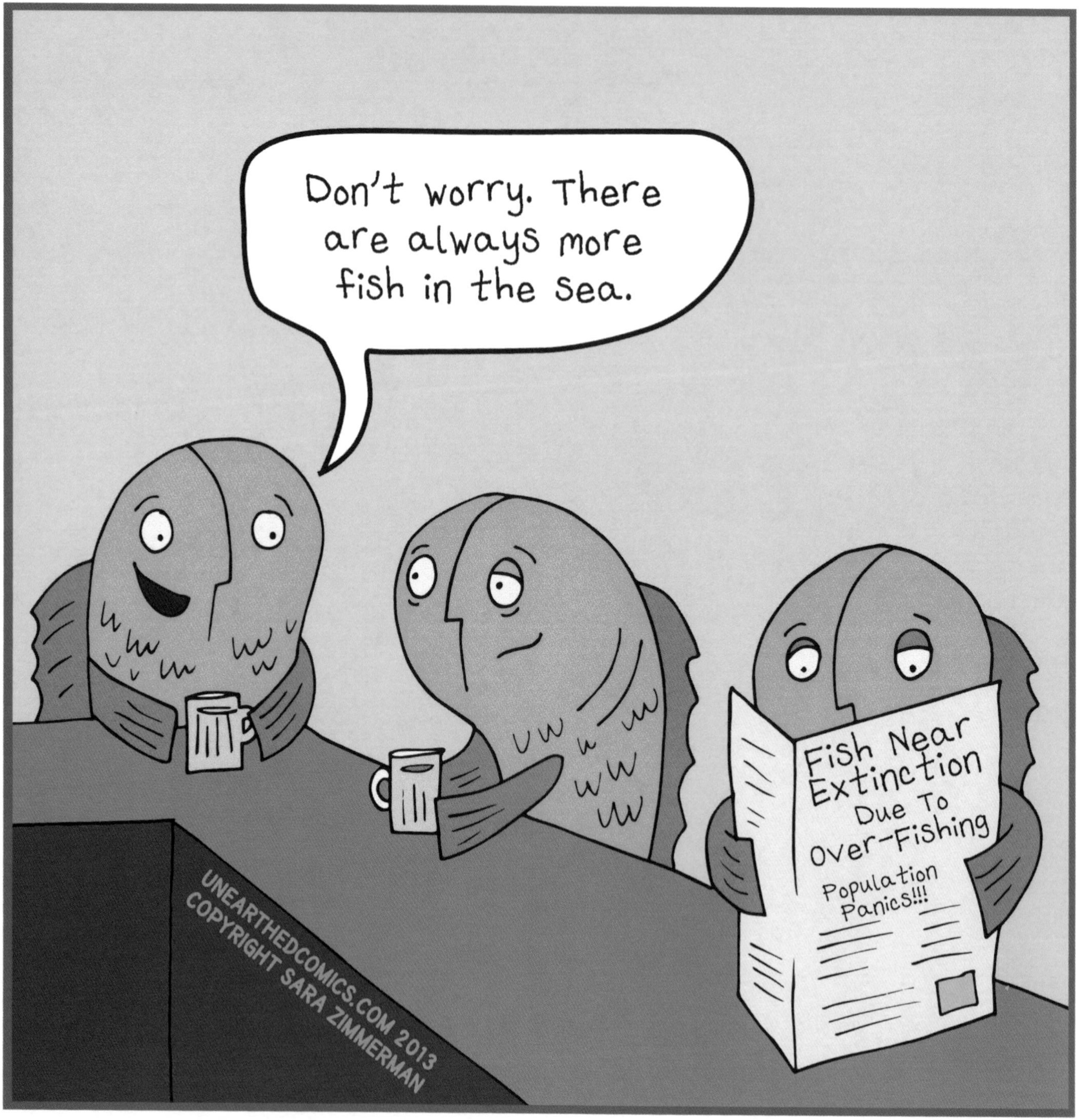
Don't worry. There are always more fish in the sea.
Fish Near Extinction Due To Over-Fishing
Population Panics!!!
UNEARTHEDCOMICS.COM 2013
COPYRIGHT SARA ZIMMERMAN

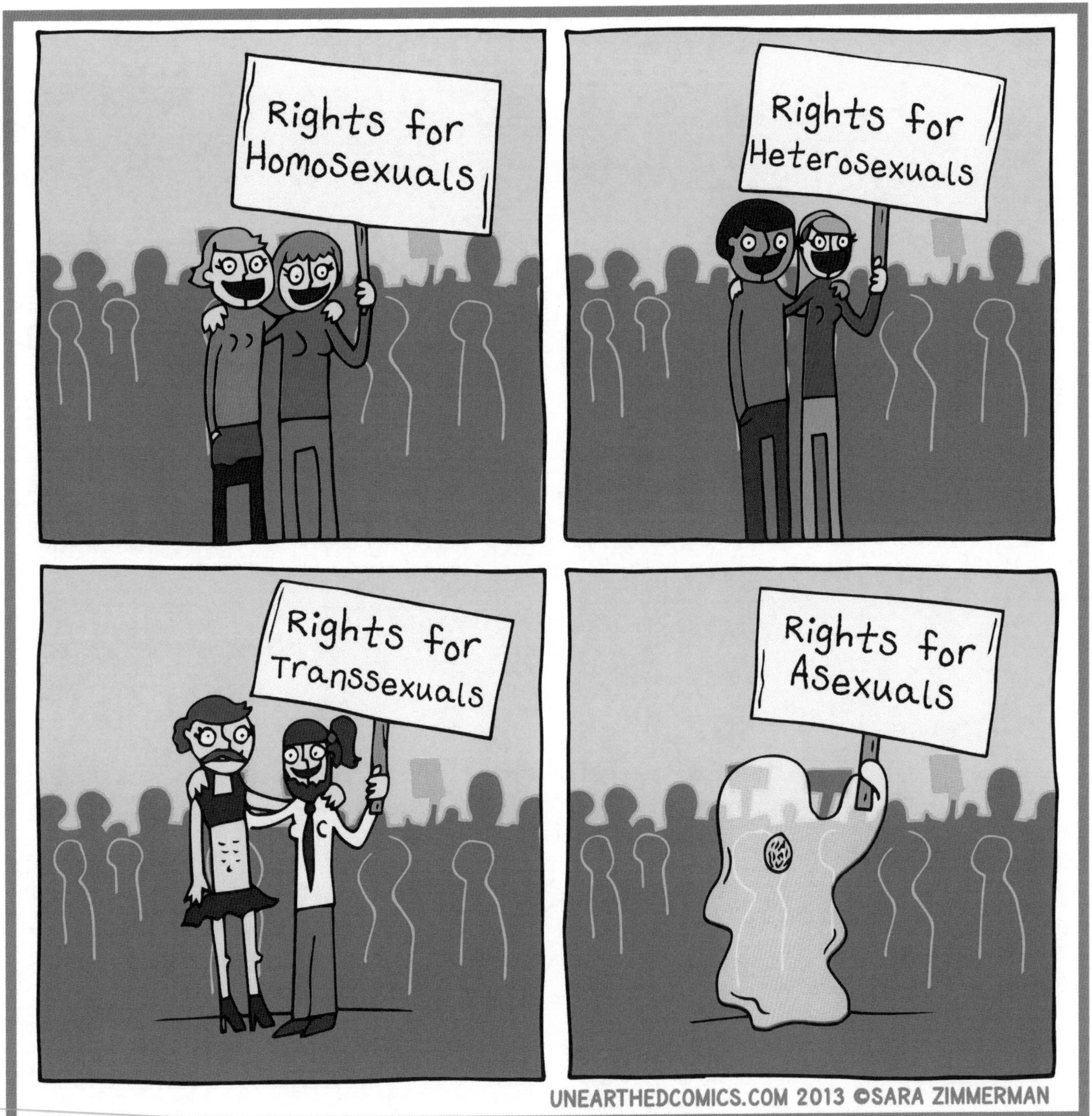
Rights for Homosexuals
Rights for Heterosexuals
Rights for Transsexuals
Rights for Asexuals
UNEARTHEDCOMICS.COM 2013 ©SARA ZIMMERMAN

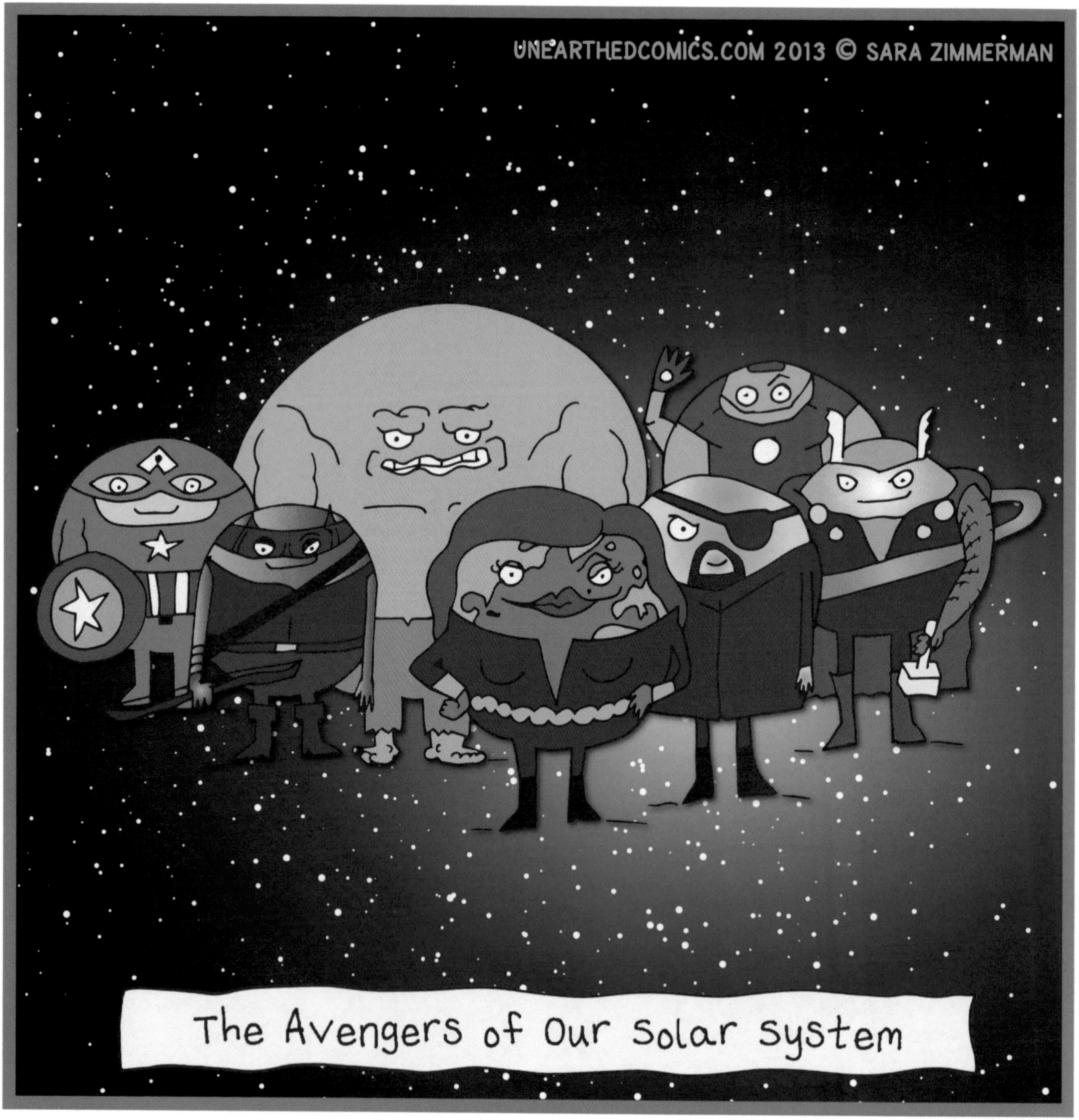
UNEARTHEDCOMICS.COM 2013 © SARA ZIMMERMAN
The Avengers of Our Solar System

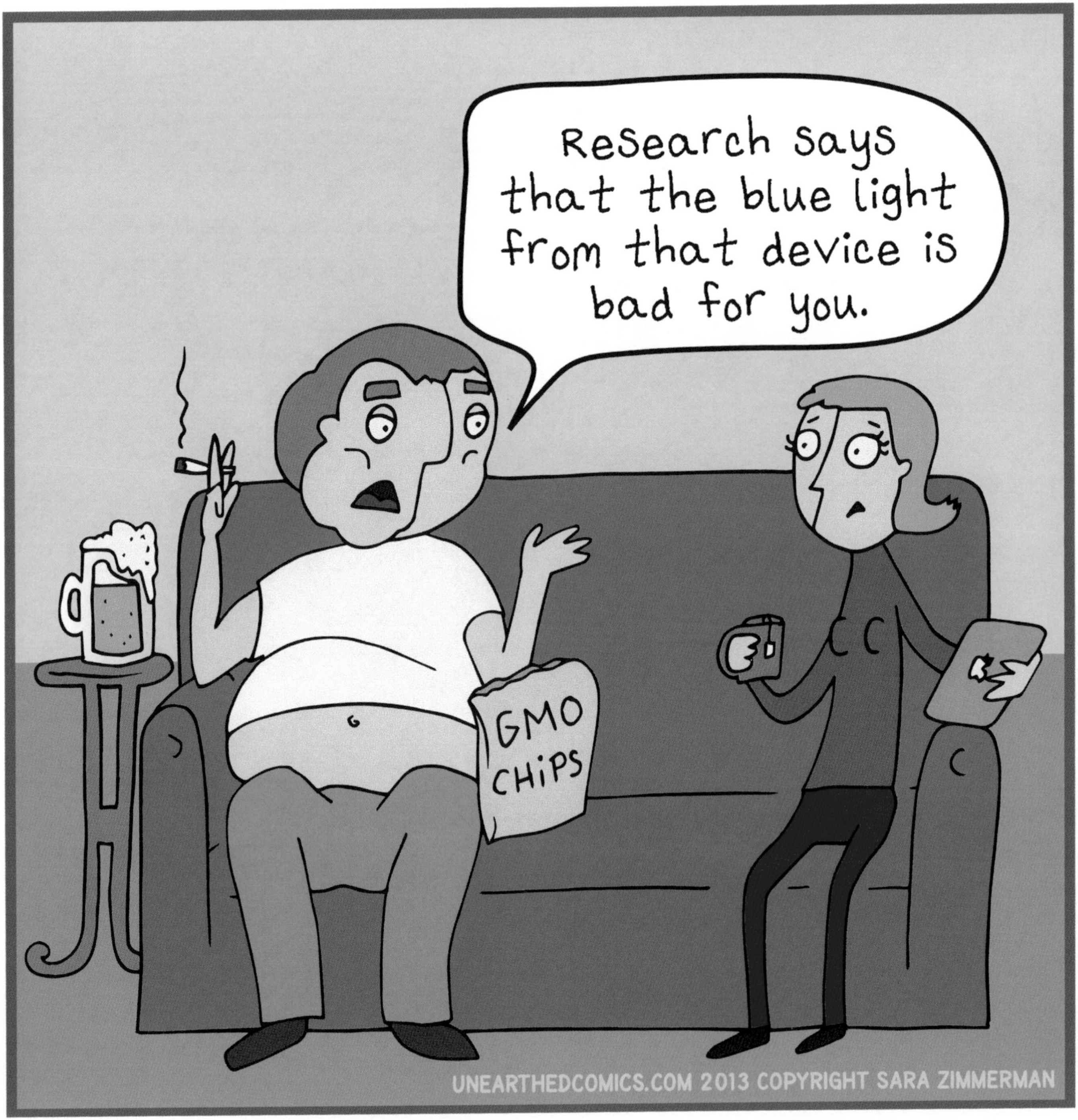
Research says that the blue light from that device is bad for you.
GMO CHiPS
UNEARTHEDCOMICS.COM 2013 COPYRIGHT SARA ZIMMERMAN

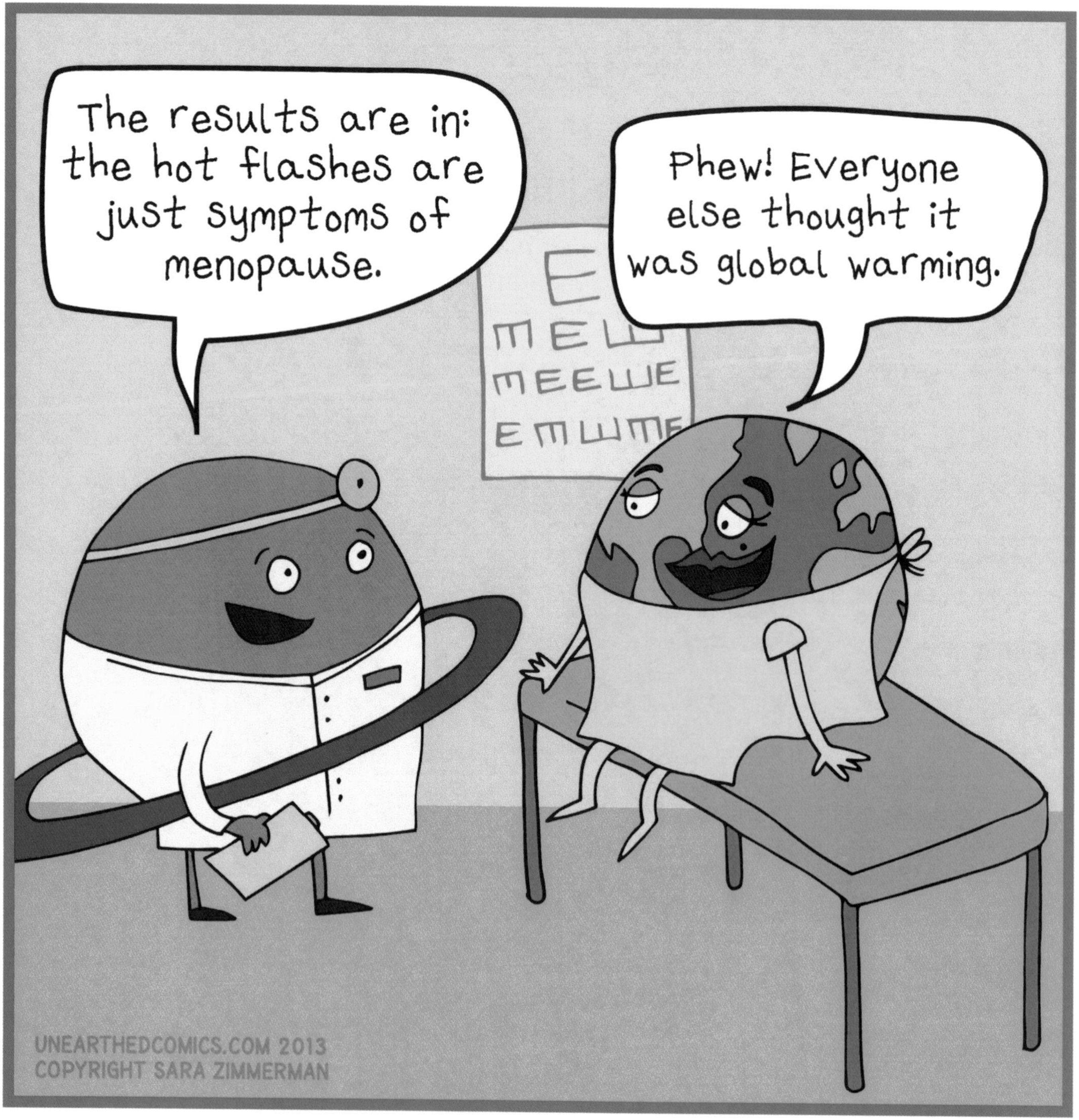

The results are in: the hot flashes are just symptoms of menopause.
Phew! Everyone else thought it was global warming.
E
MEW
MEEWE
EMWME
UNEARTHEDCOMICS.COM 2013
COPYRIGHT SARA ZIMMERMAN

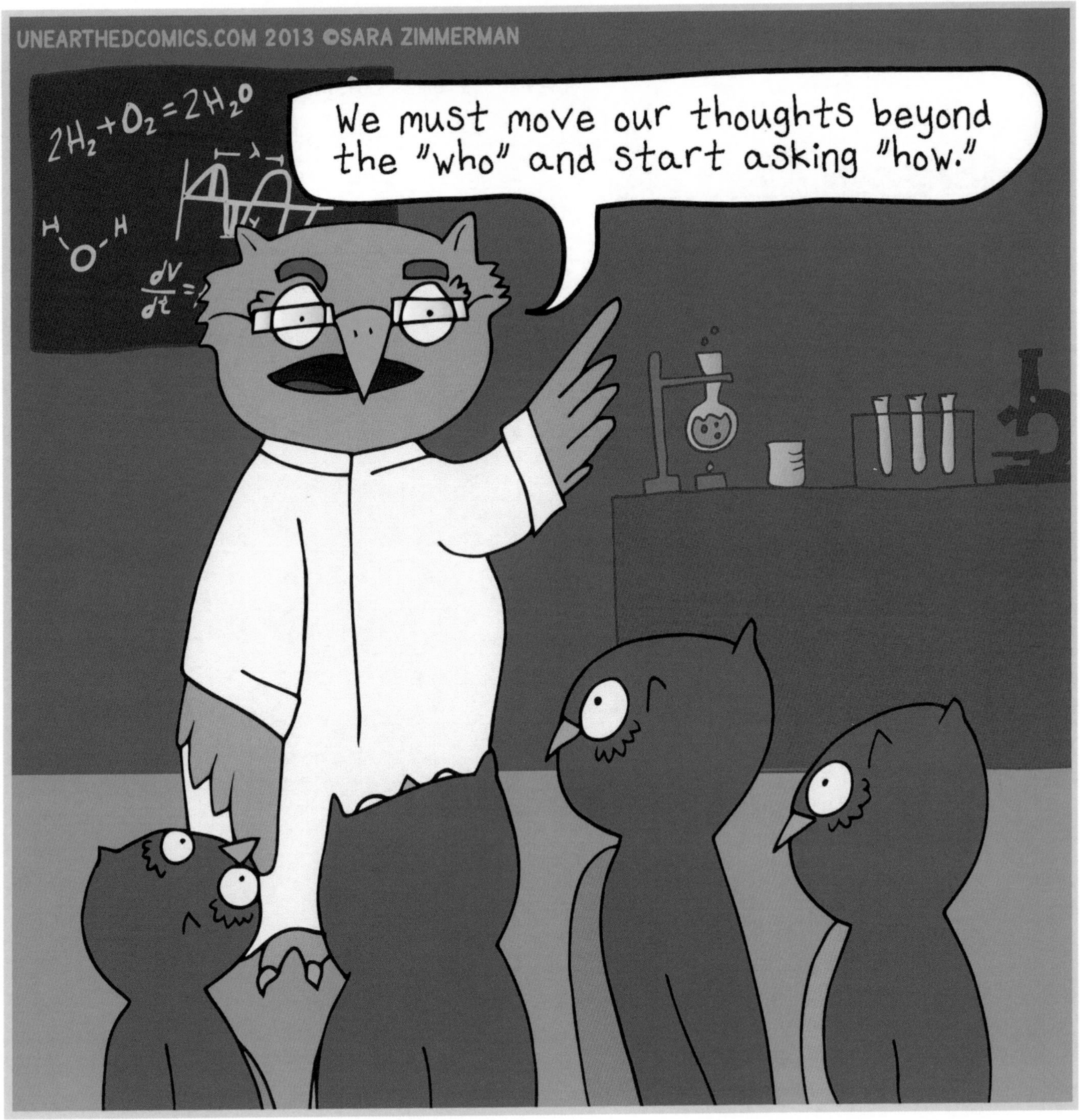
UNEARTHEDCOMICS.COM 2013 ©SARA ZIMMERMAN
$2H_2 + O_2 = 2H_2O$
We must move our thoughts beyond the "who" and start asking "how."

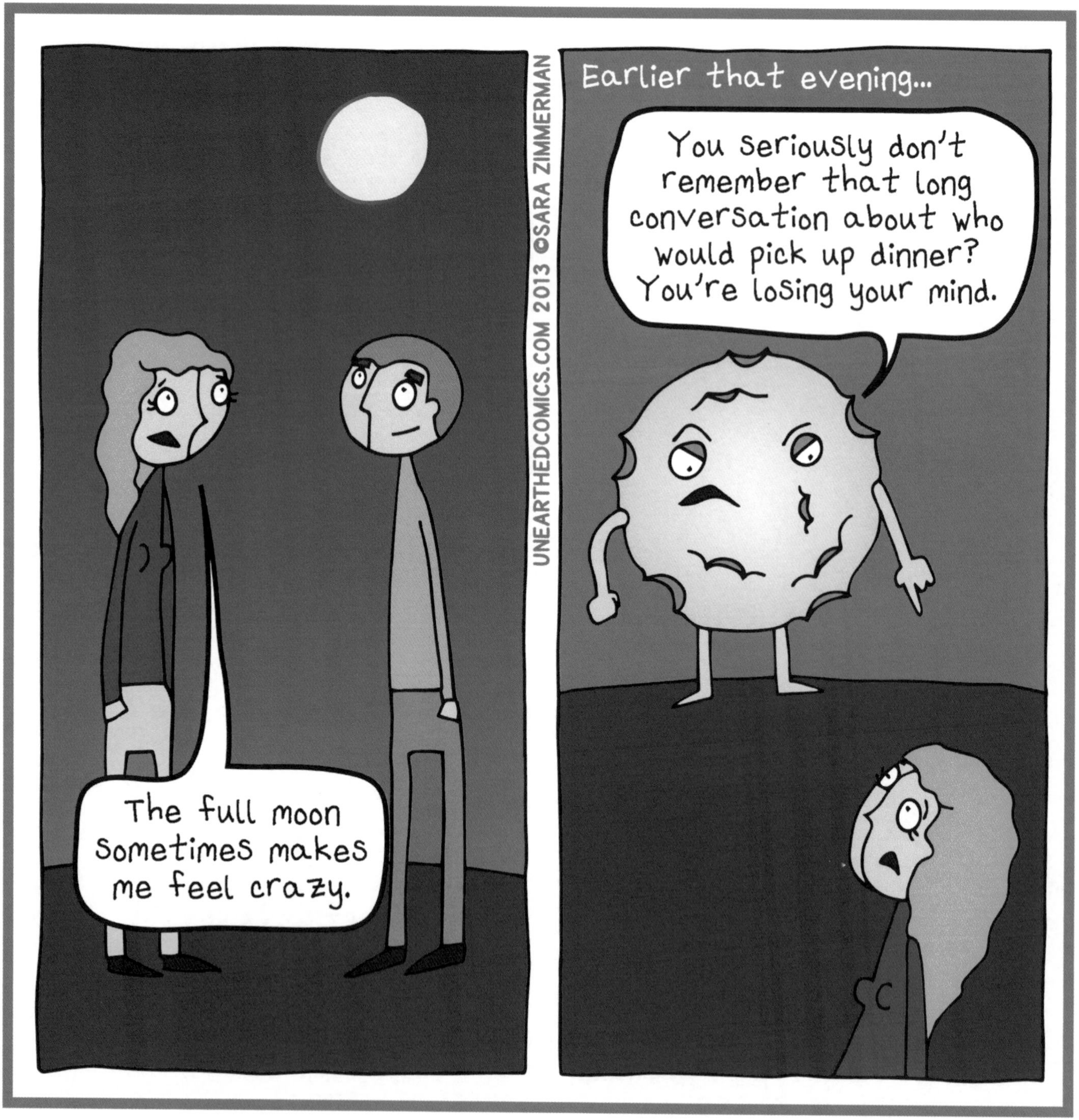
The full moon sometimes makes me feel crazy.
UNEARTHEDCOMICS.COM 2013 ©SARA ZIMMERMAN
Earlier that evening...
You seriously don't remember that long conversation about who would pick up dinner? You're losing your mind.

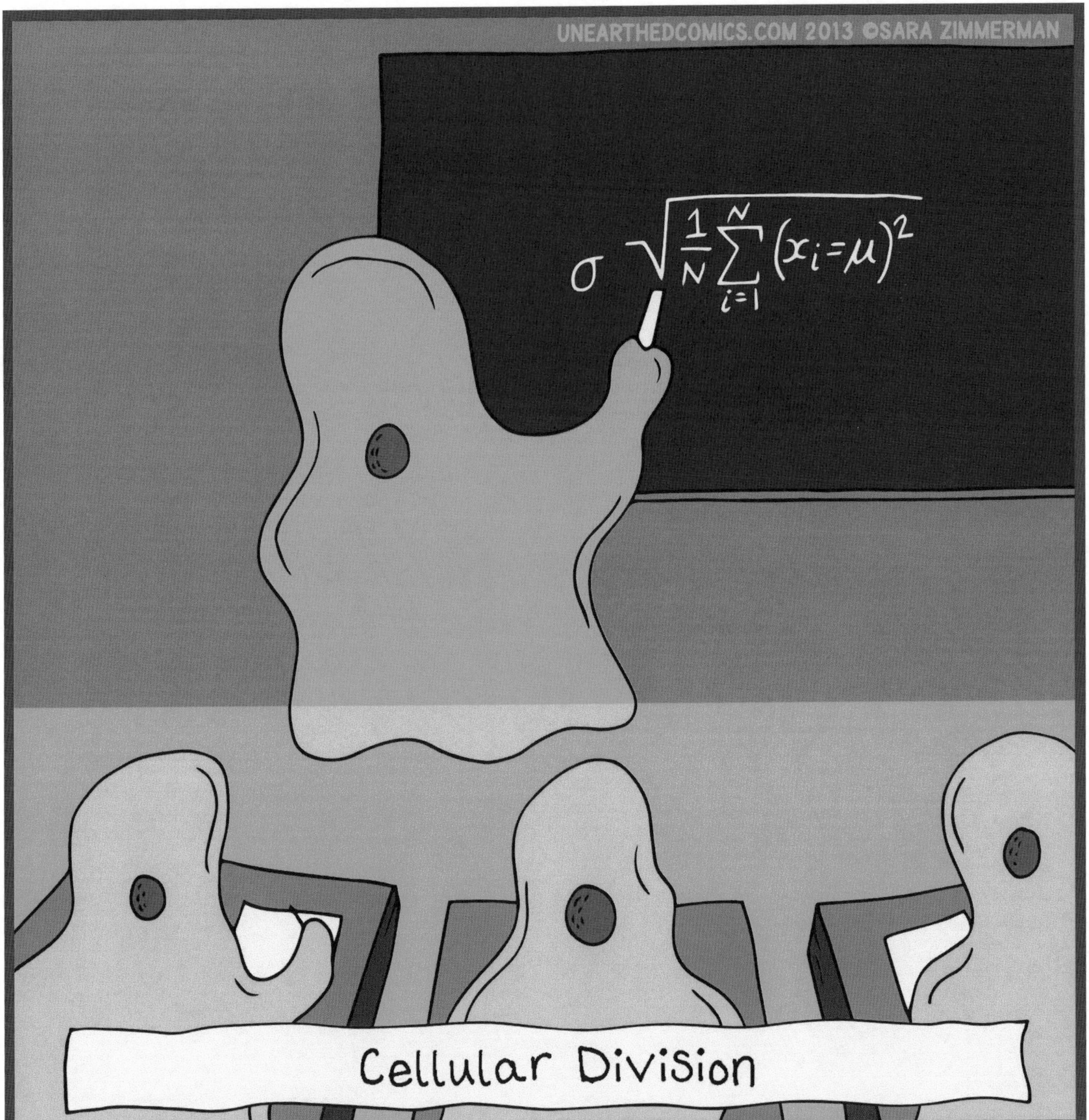
UNEARTHEDCOMICS.COM 2013 ©SARA ZIMMERMAN
$\sigma \sqrt{\frac{1}{N}\sum_{i=1}^{N}(x_i = \mu)^2}$
Cellular Division

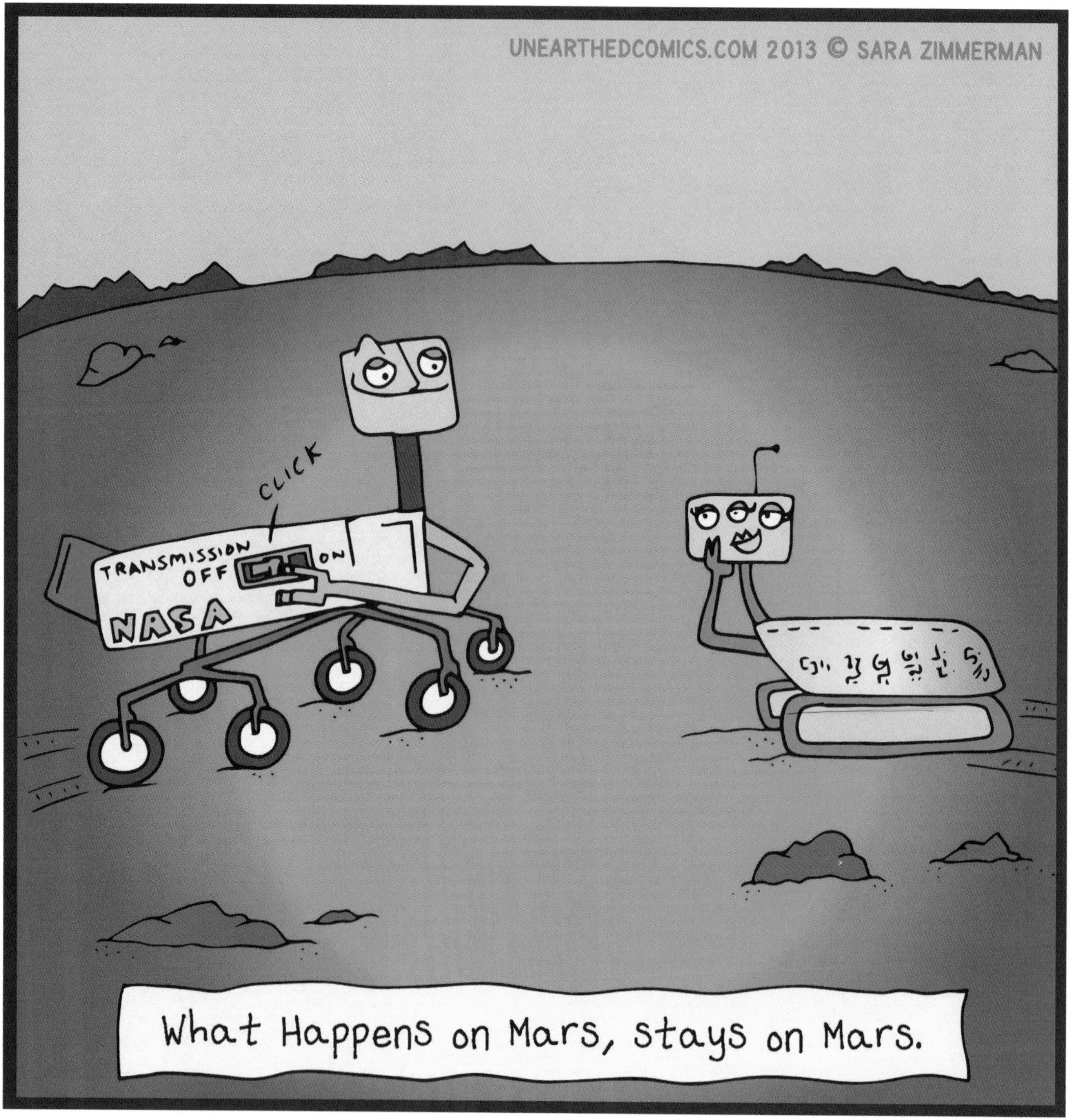
UNEARTHEDCOMICS.COM 2013 © SARA ZIMMERMAN
CLICK
TRANSMISSION
OFF
ON
NASA
What Happens on Mars, stays on Mars.

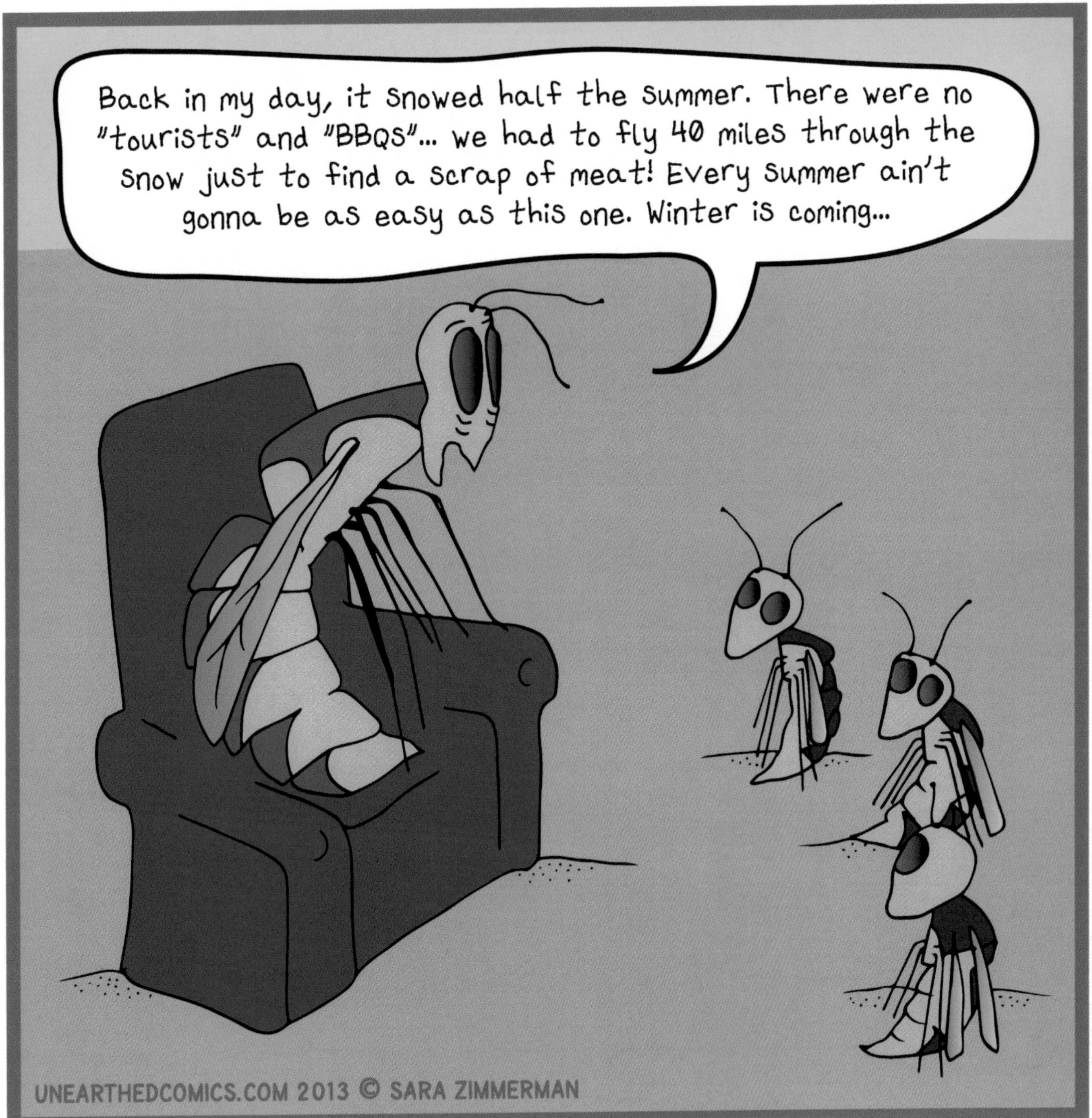
Back in my day, it snowed half the summer. There were no "tourists" and "BBQS"... we had to fly 40 miles through the snow just to find a scrap of meat! Every summer ain't gonna be as easy as this one. Winter is coming...
UNEARTHEDCOMICS.COM 2013 © SARA ZIMMERMAN

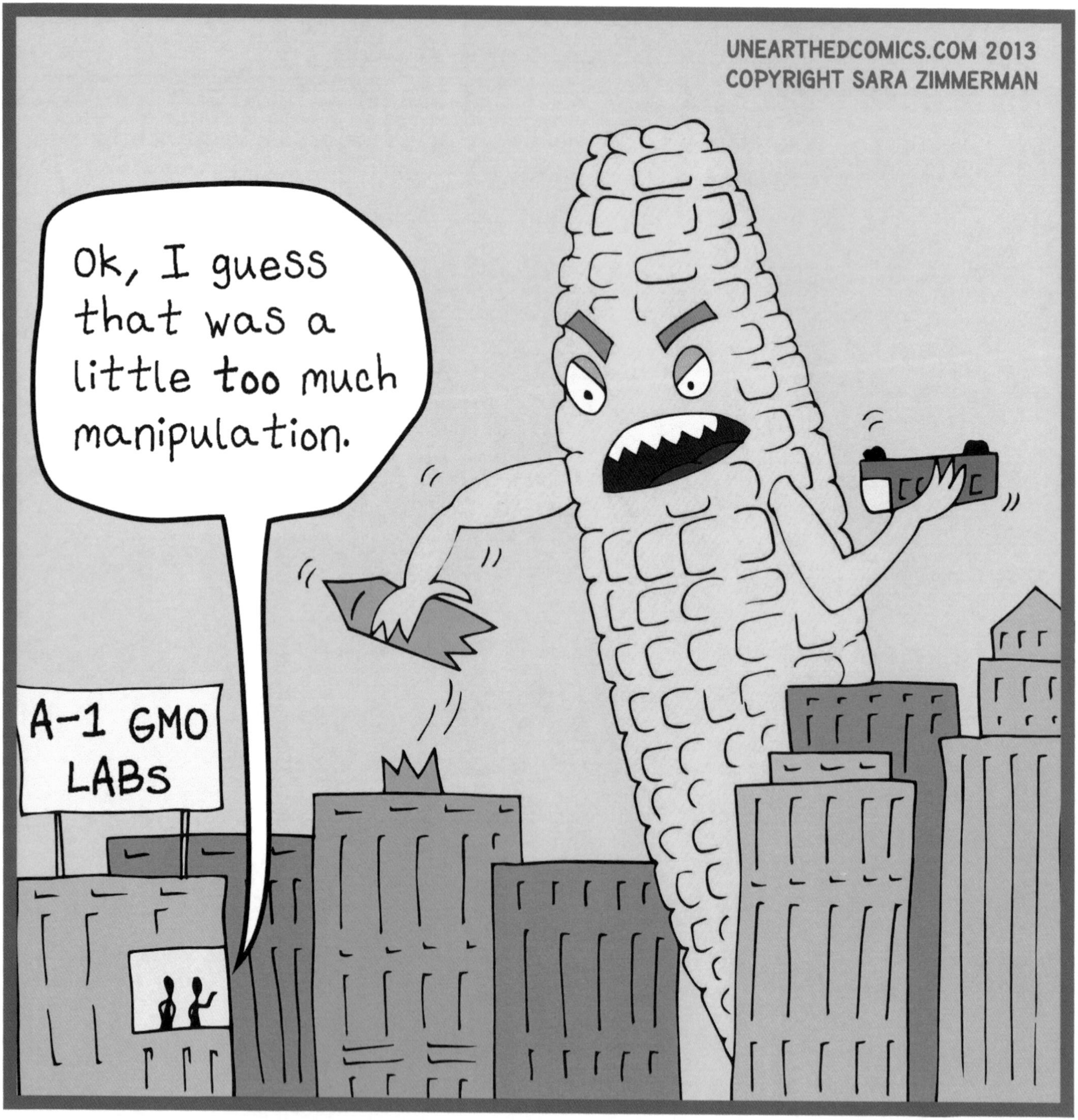

UNEARTHEDCOMICS.COM 2013
COPYRIGHT SARA ZIMMERMAN
Ok, I guess that was a little too much manipulation.
A-1 GMO LABS

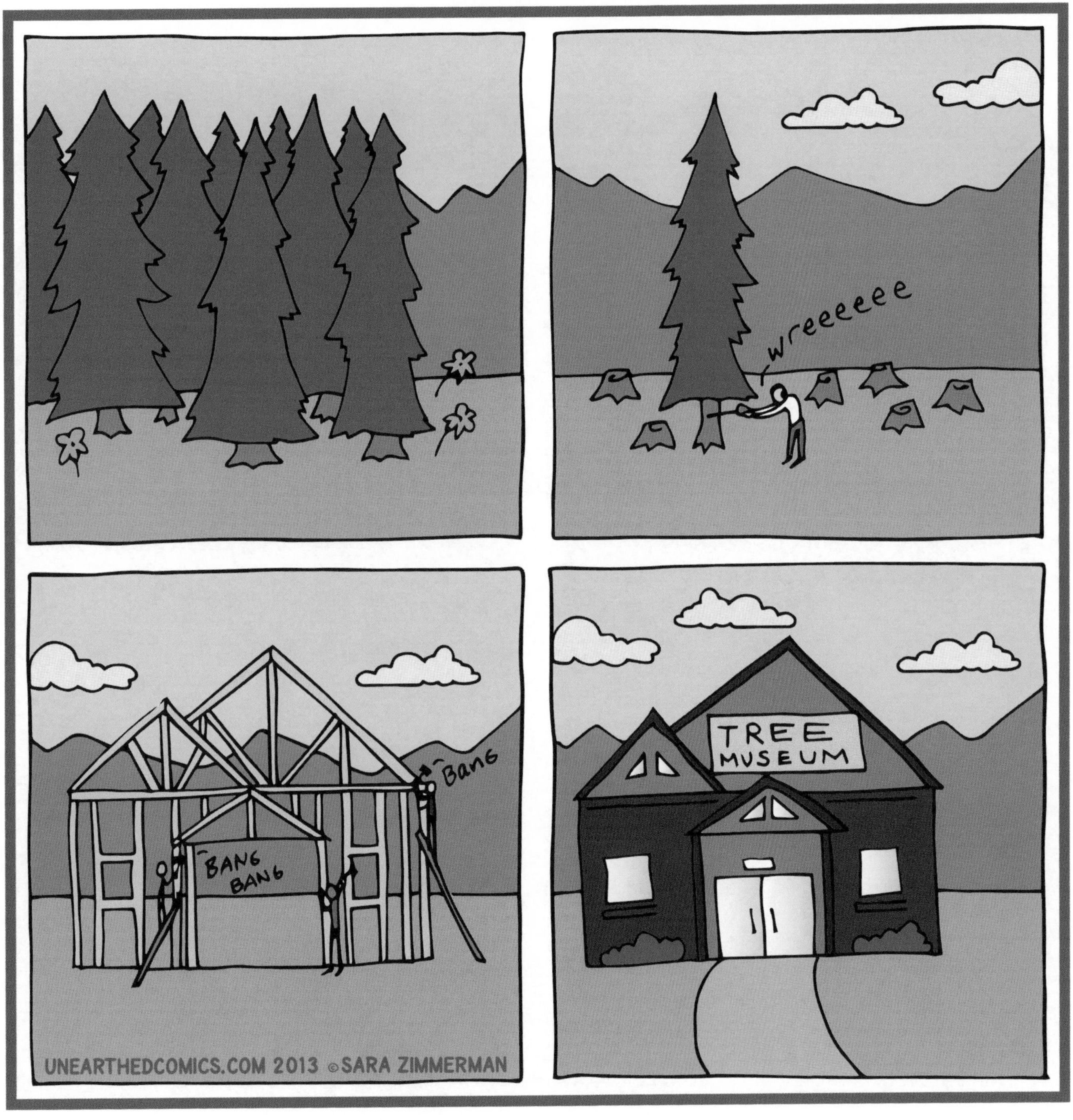
wreeeeee
BANG
BANG
Bang
UNEARTHEDCOMICS.COM 2013 ©SARA ZIMMERMAN
TREE
MUSEUM

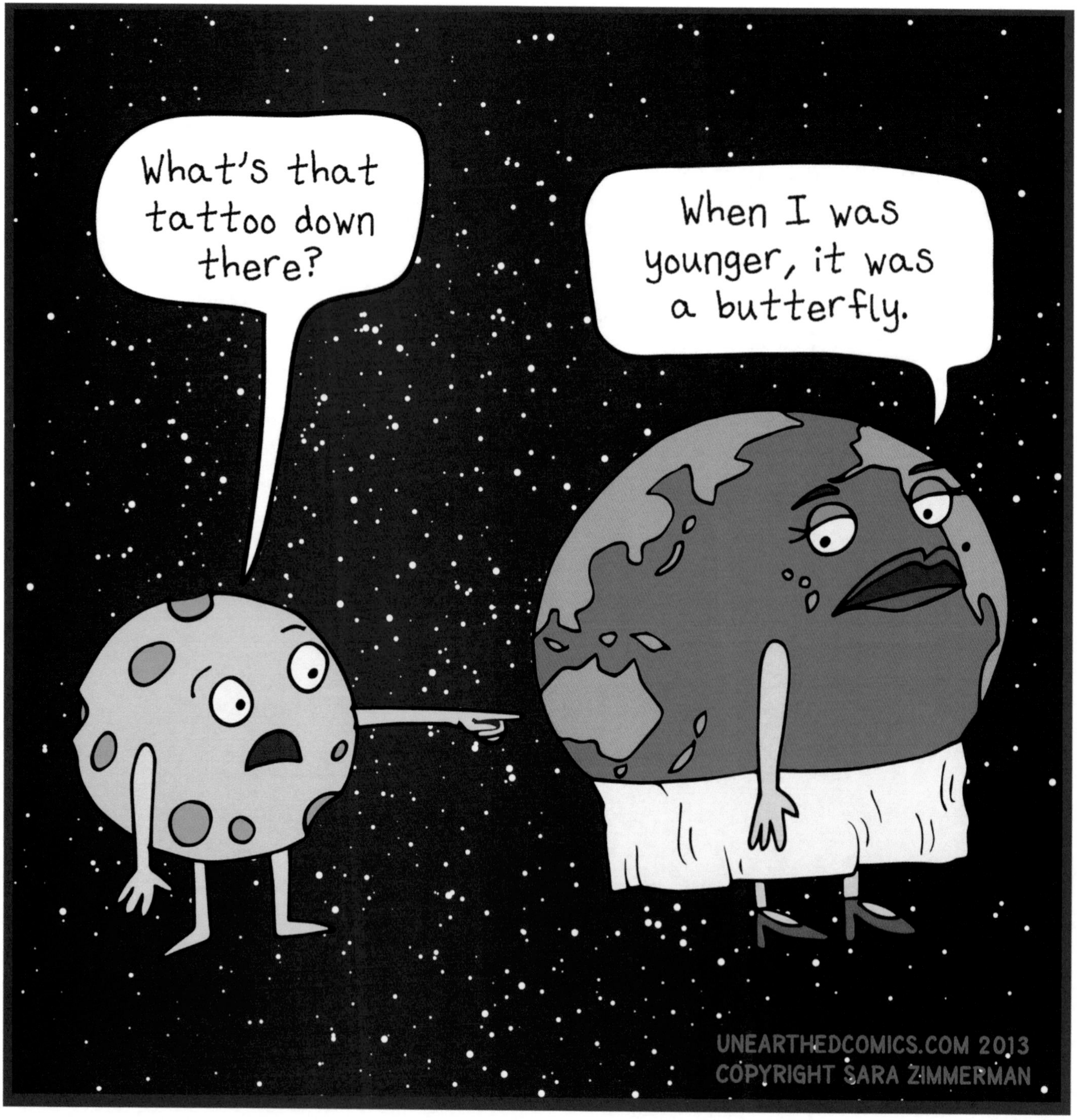
What's that tattoo down there?
When I was younger, it was a butterfly.
UNEARTHEDCOMICS.COM 2013
COPYRIGHT SARA ZIMMERMAN

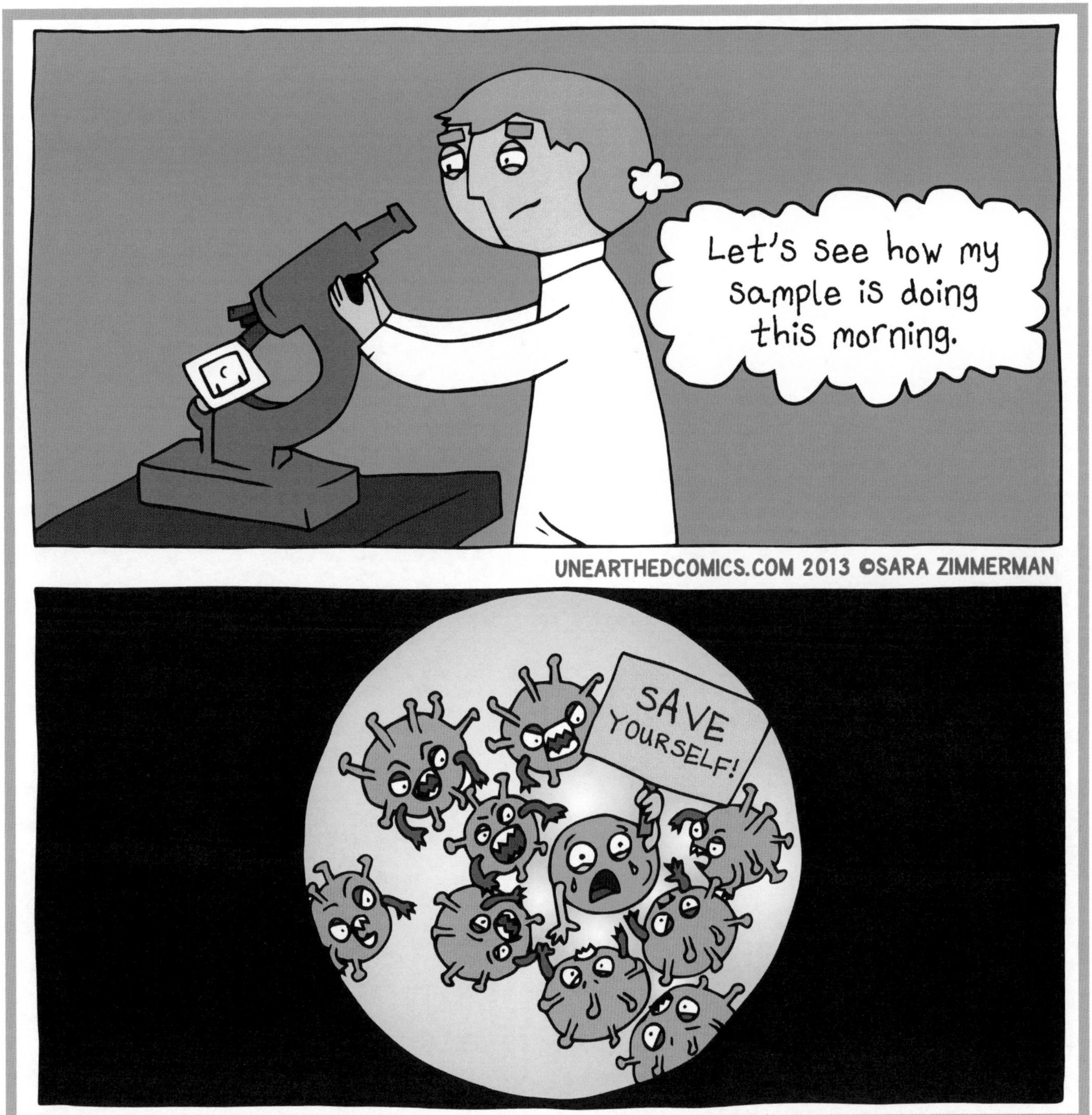
Let's see how my sample is doing this morning.
UNEARTHEDCOMICS.COM 2013 ©SARA ZIMMERMAN
SAVE YOURSELF!

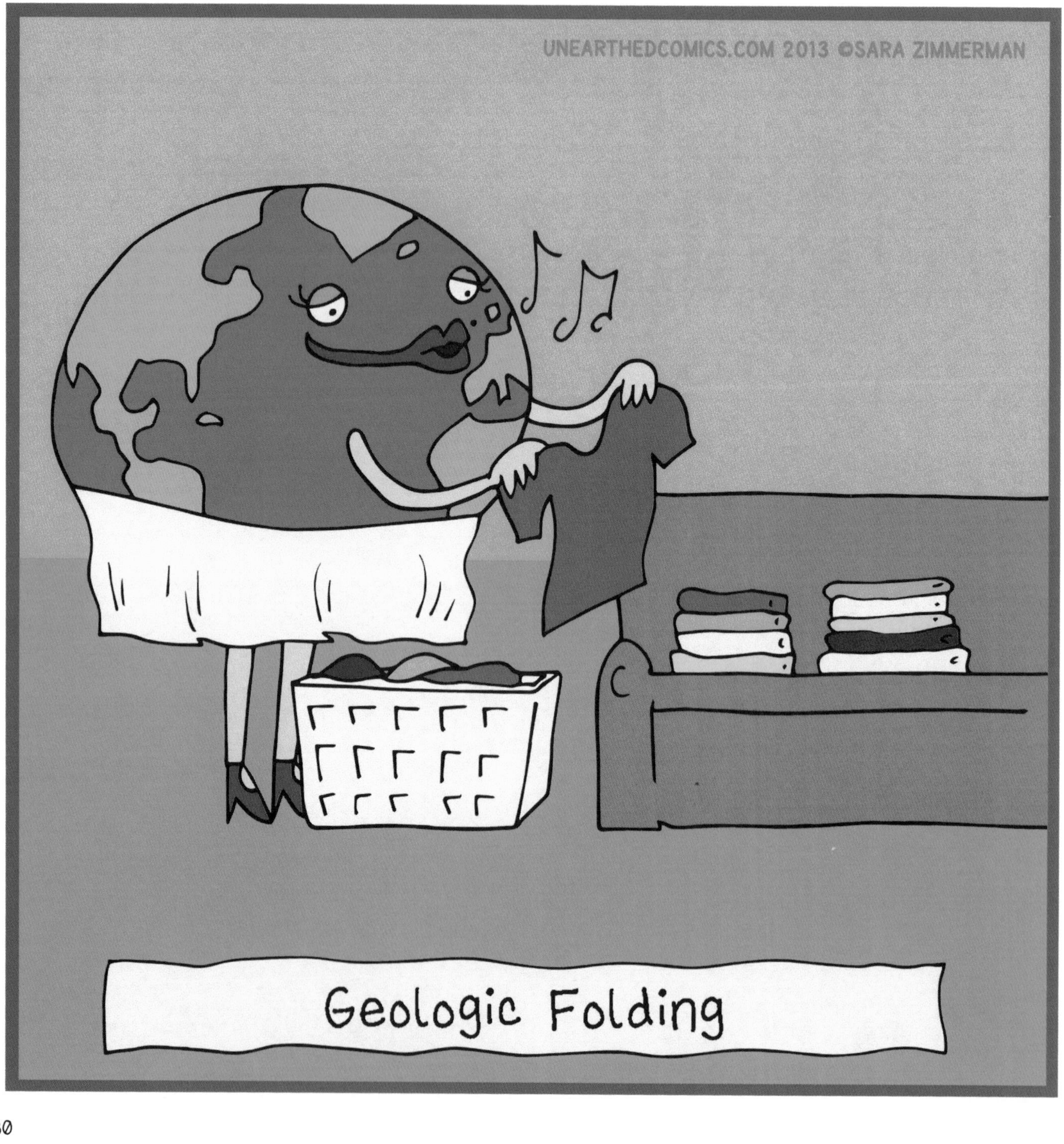
UNEARTHEDCOMICS.COM 2013 ©SARA ZIMMERMAN
Geologic Folding

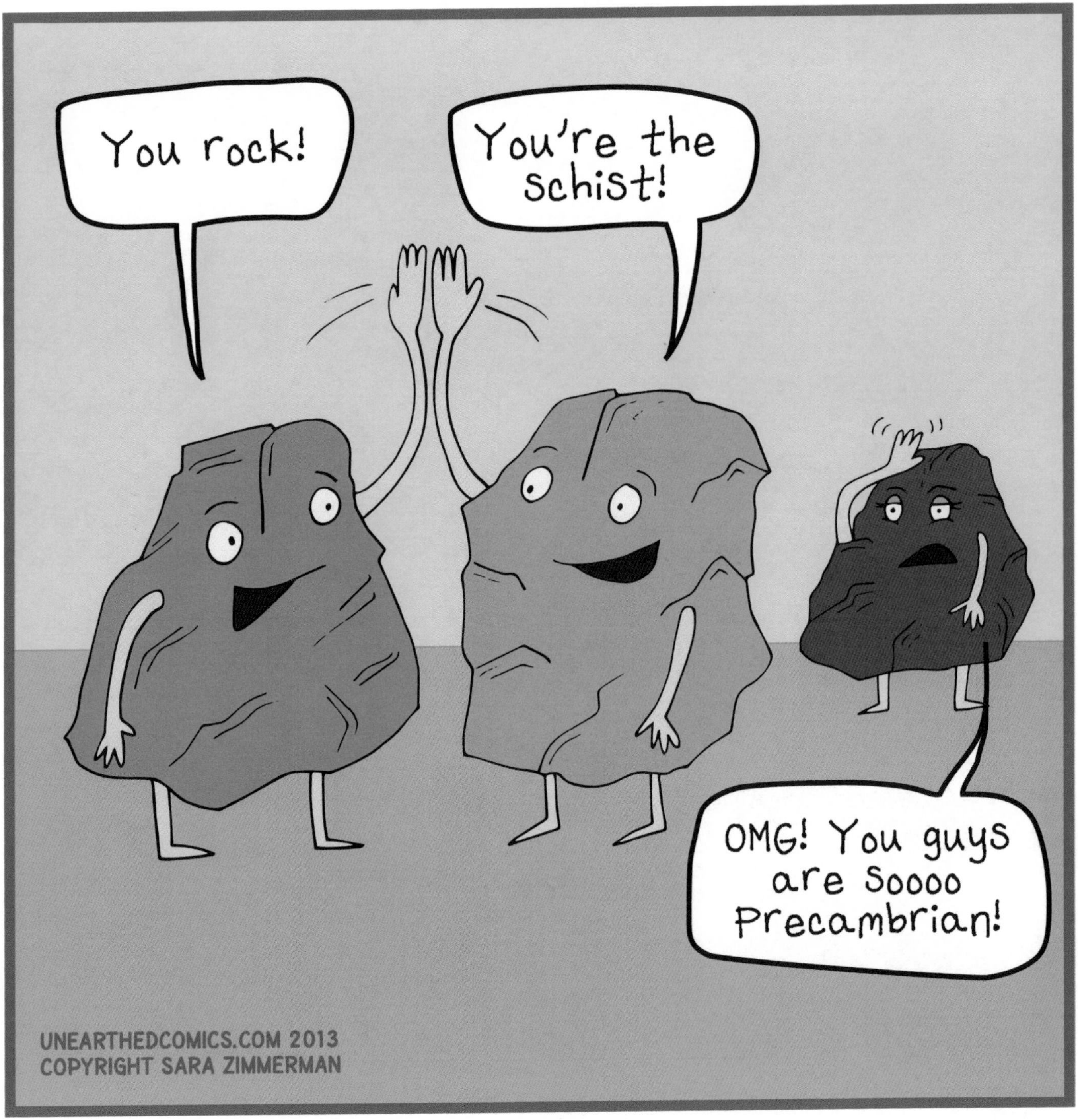
You rock!
You're the schist!
OMG! You guys are Soooo Precambrian!
UNEARTHEDCOMICS.COM 2013
COPYRIGHT SARA ZIMMERMAN

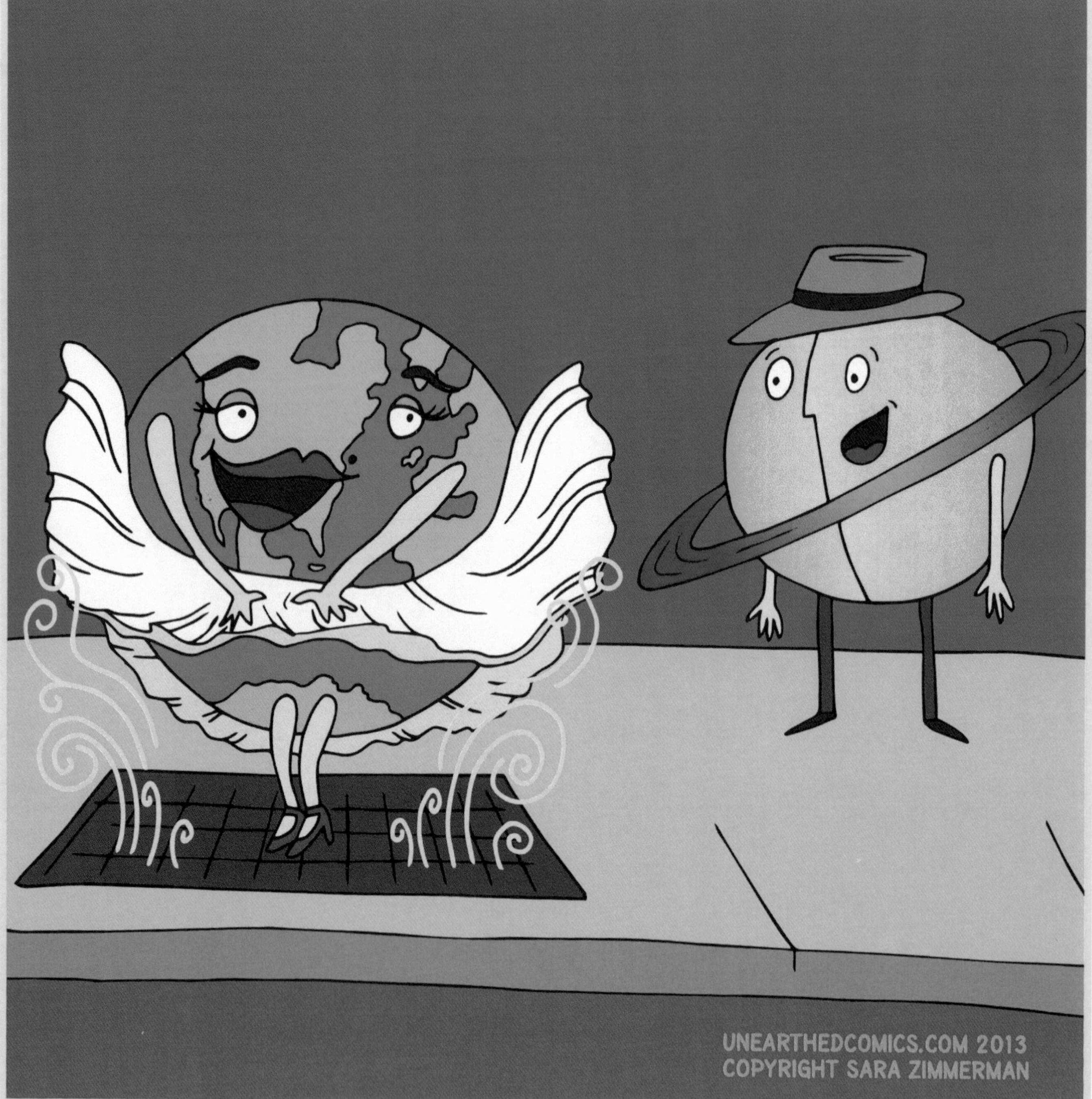
UNEARTHEDCOMICS.COM 2013
COPYRIGHT SARA ZIMMERMAN

Along with my comics, I tell my story through art, graphic/web design, and illustration.
Here are some of my artworks about the world around us:

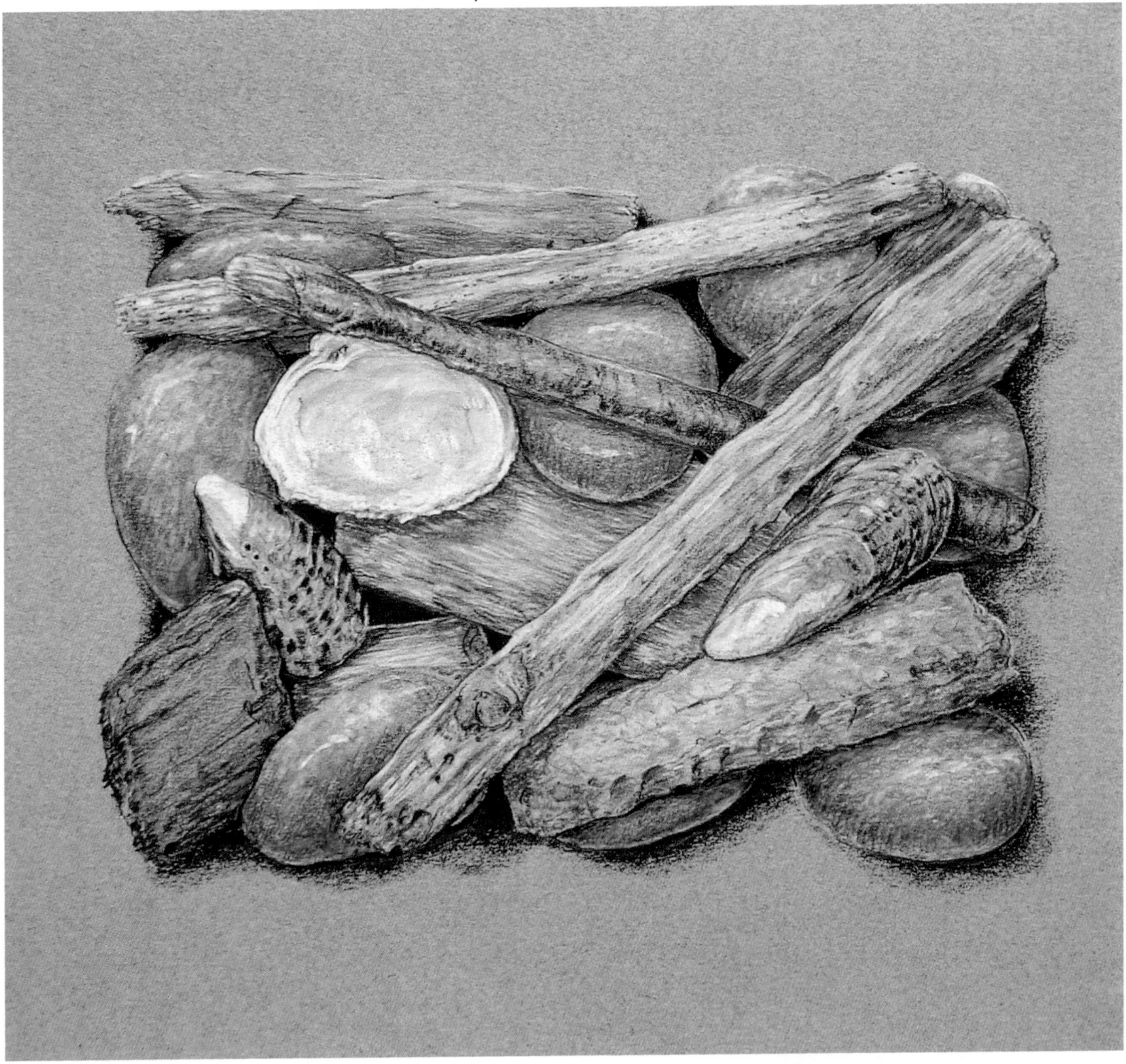

"After A Storm," colored pencil on paper

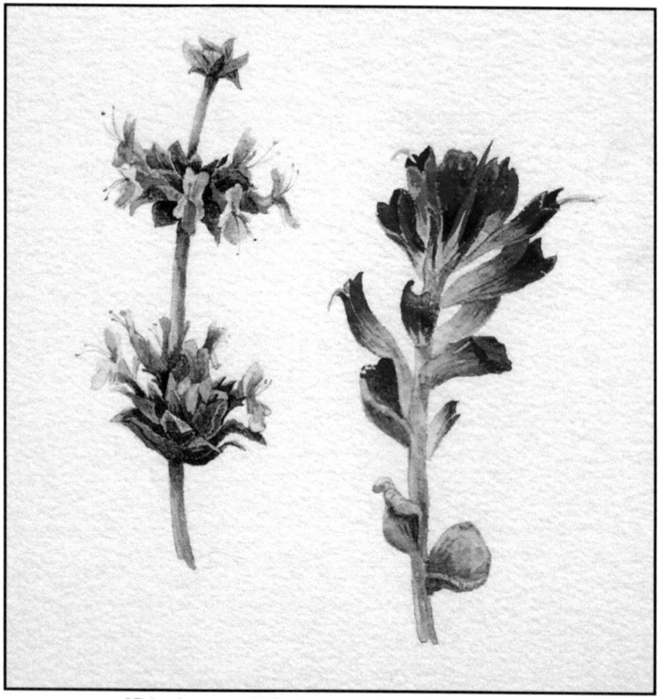

"Black sage & Indian paintbrush" watercolor on paper

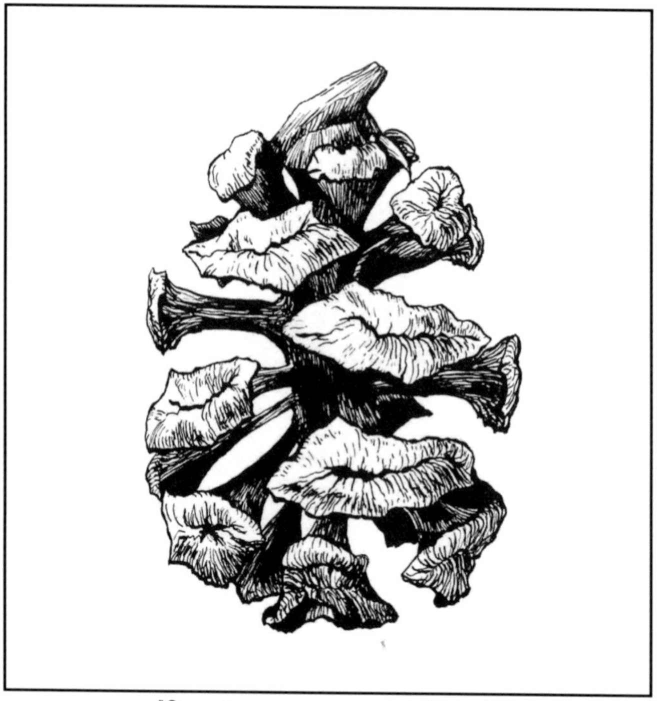

"Sequoia sempervirens seed cone" ink on clayboard

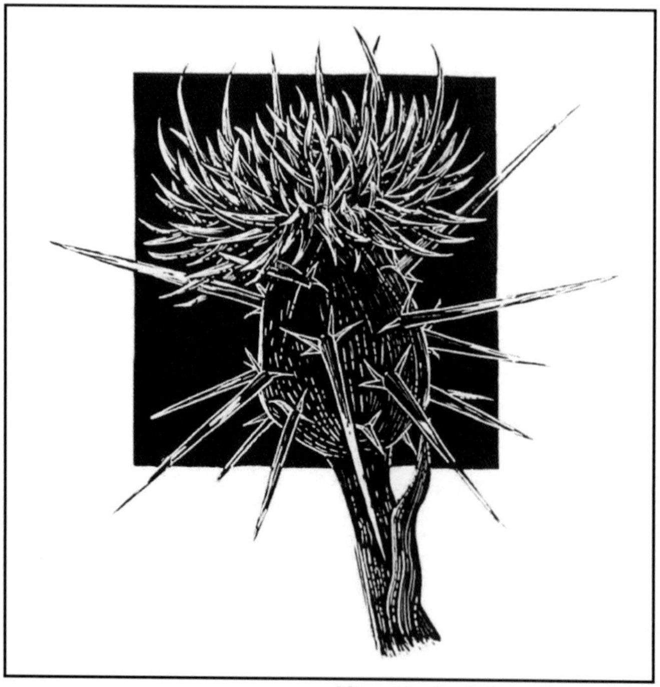

"Star thistle," ink on clayboard

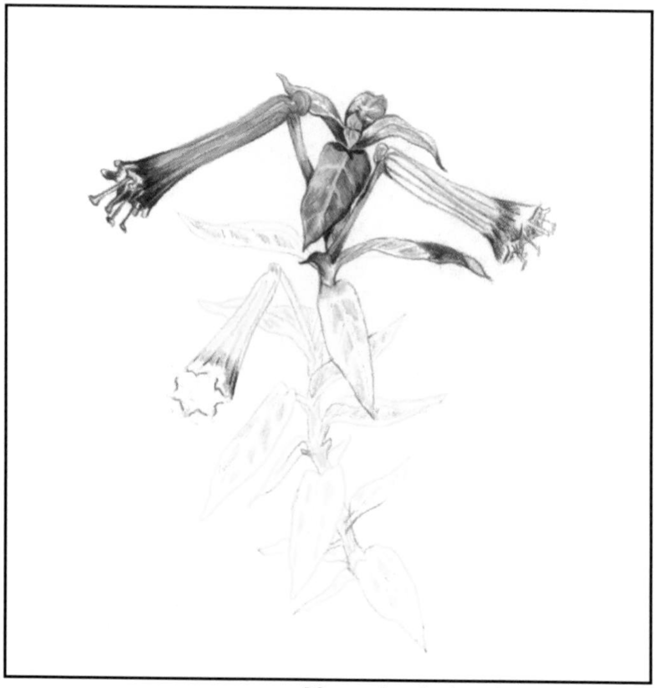

"Cigar plant" colored pencil on paper

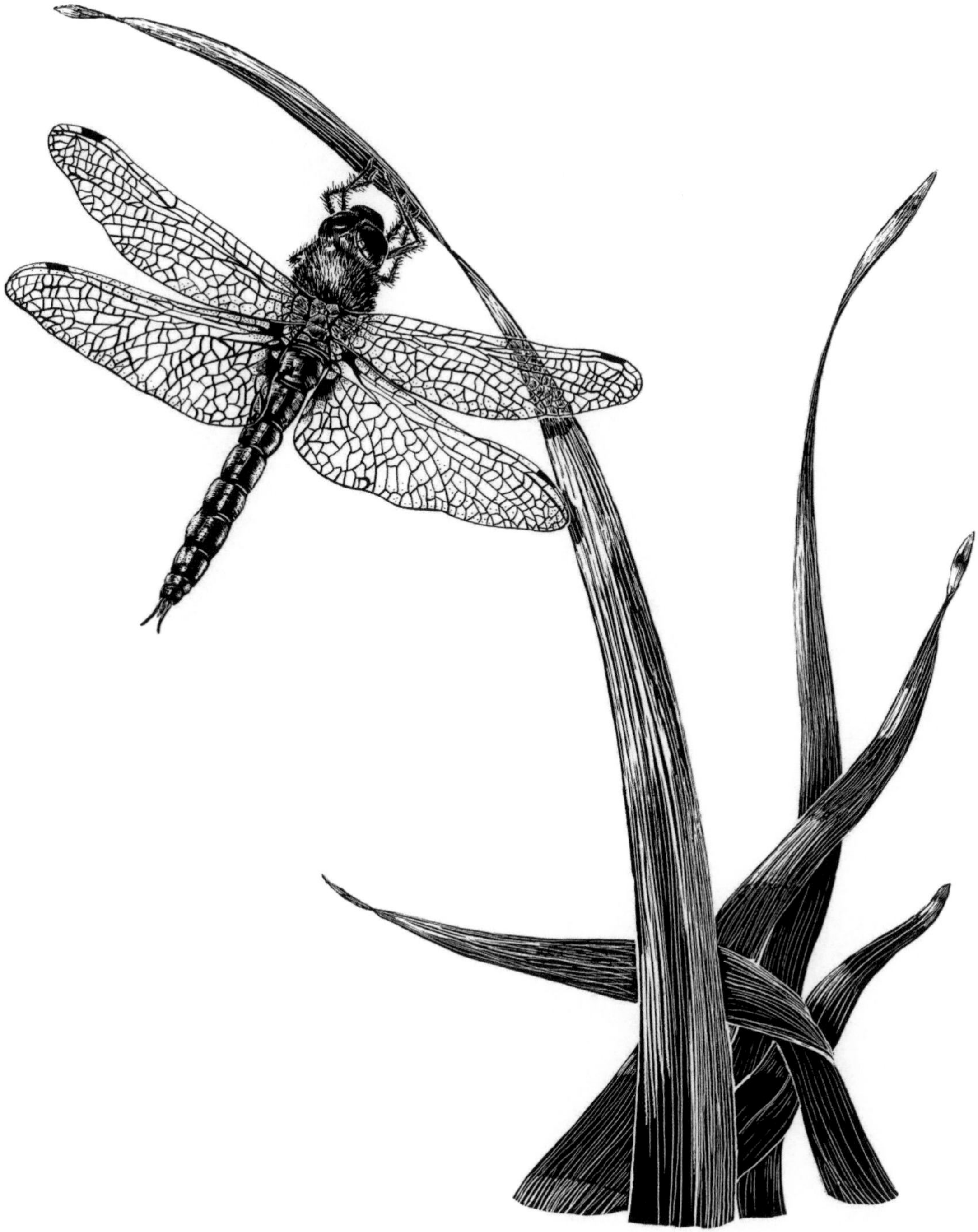

"*Epitheca cynosaura,*" ink on clayboard

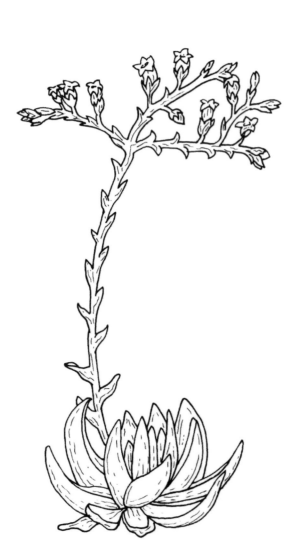

"Sea lettuce," pen on paper

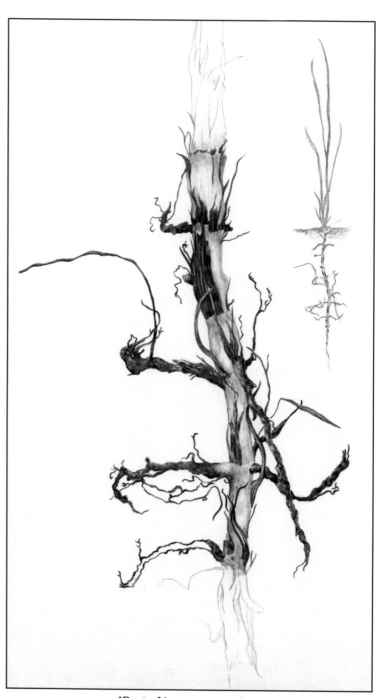

"Root of Leymus triticoides" colored pencil on paper

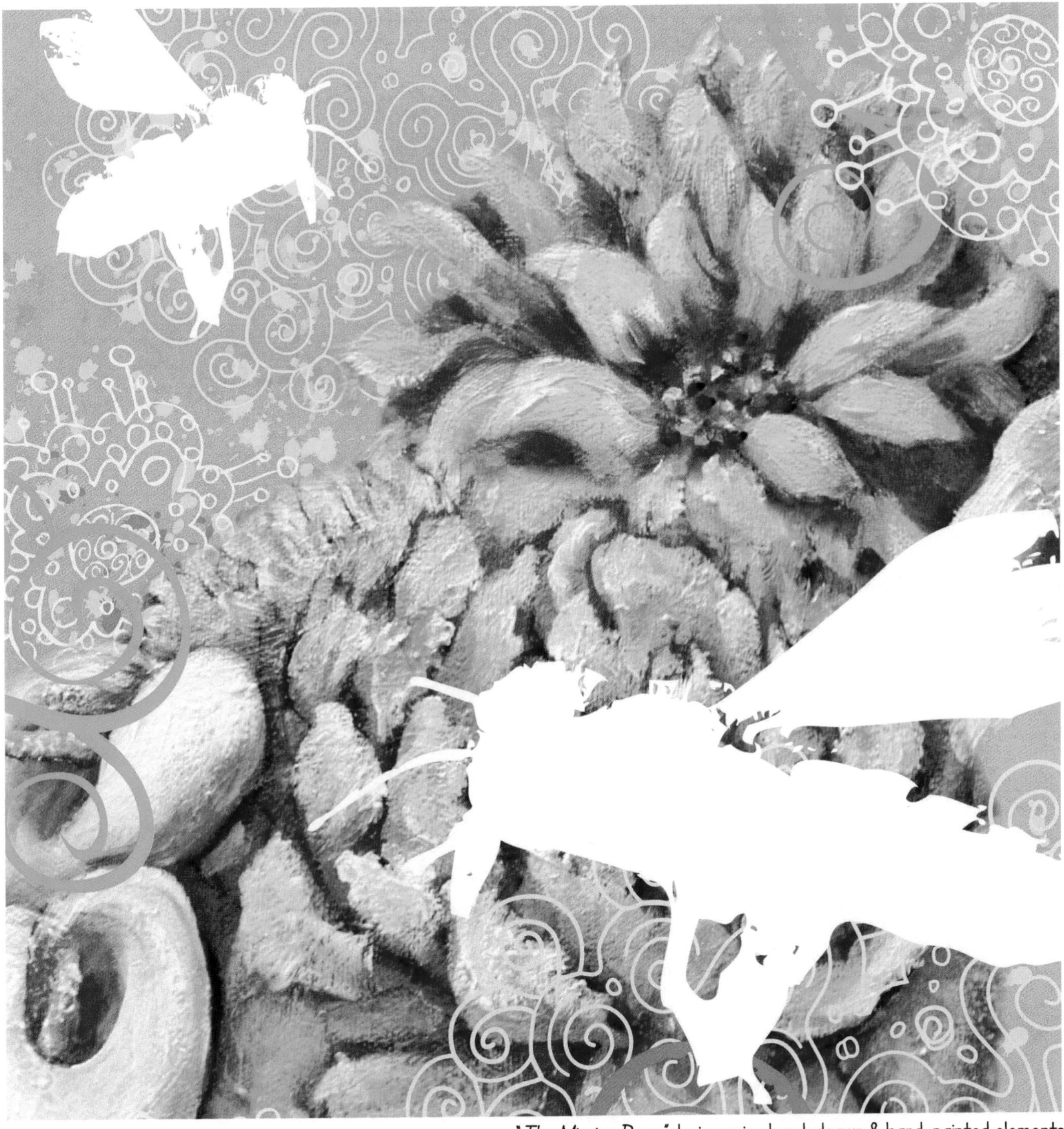

"*The Missing Bees*" design using hand-drawn & hand-painted elements

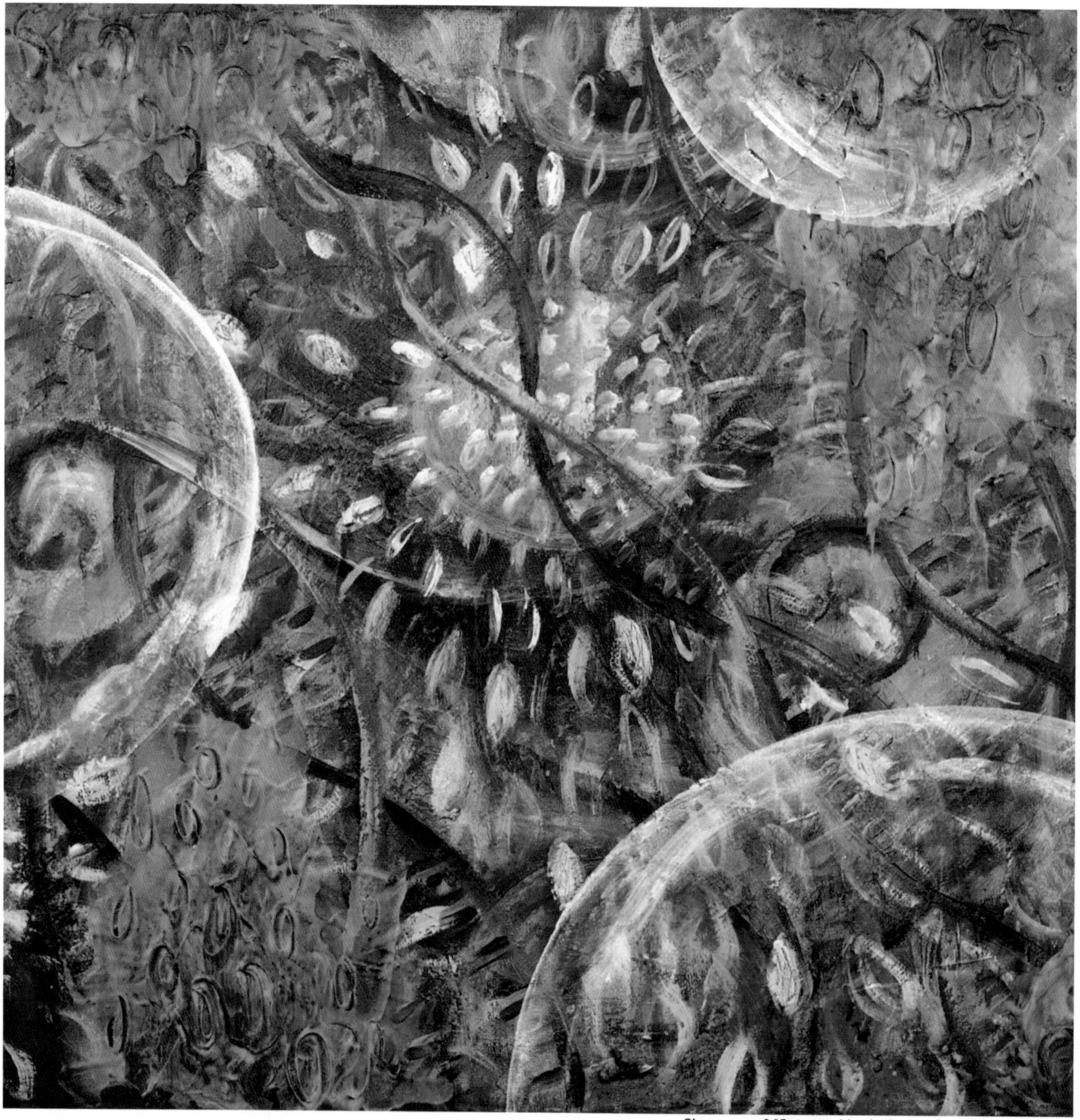

Close up of *"Internal Light"* mixed media on canvas

Here are a few comics from some of my friends.

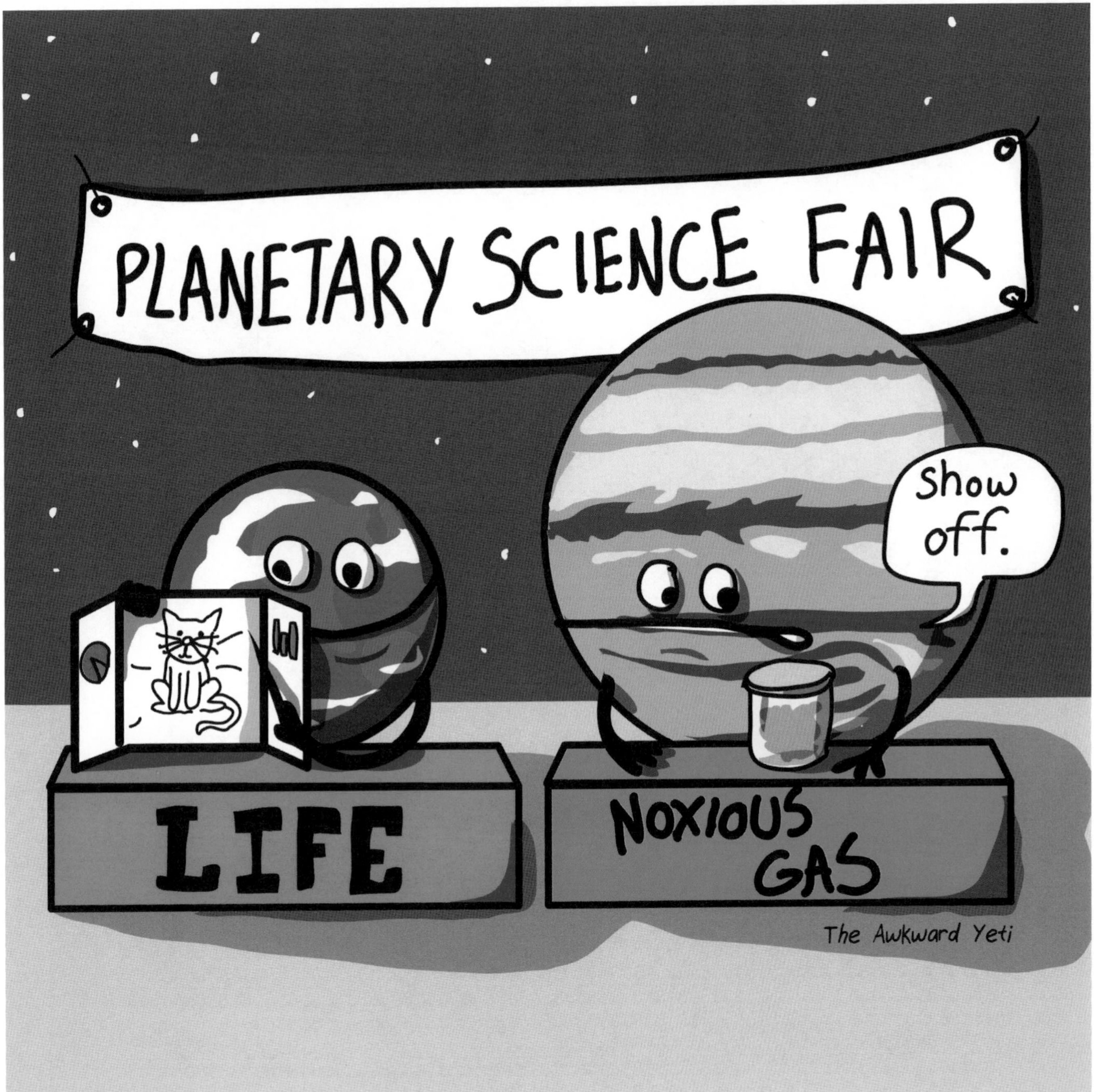
PLANETARY SCIENCE FAIR
Show off.
LIFE
NOXIOUS GAS
The Awkward Yeti

From The Awkward Yeti (awkwardyeti.com)

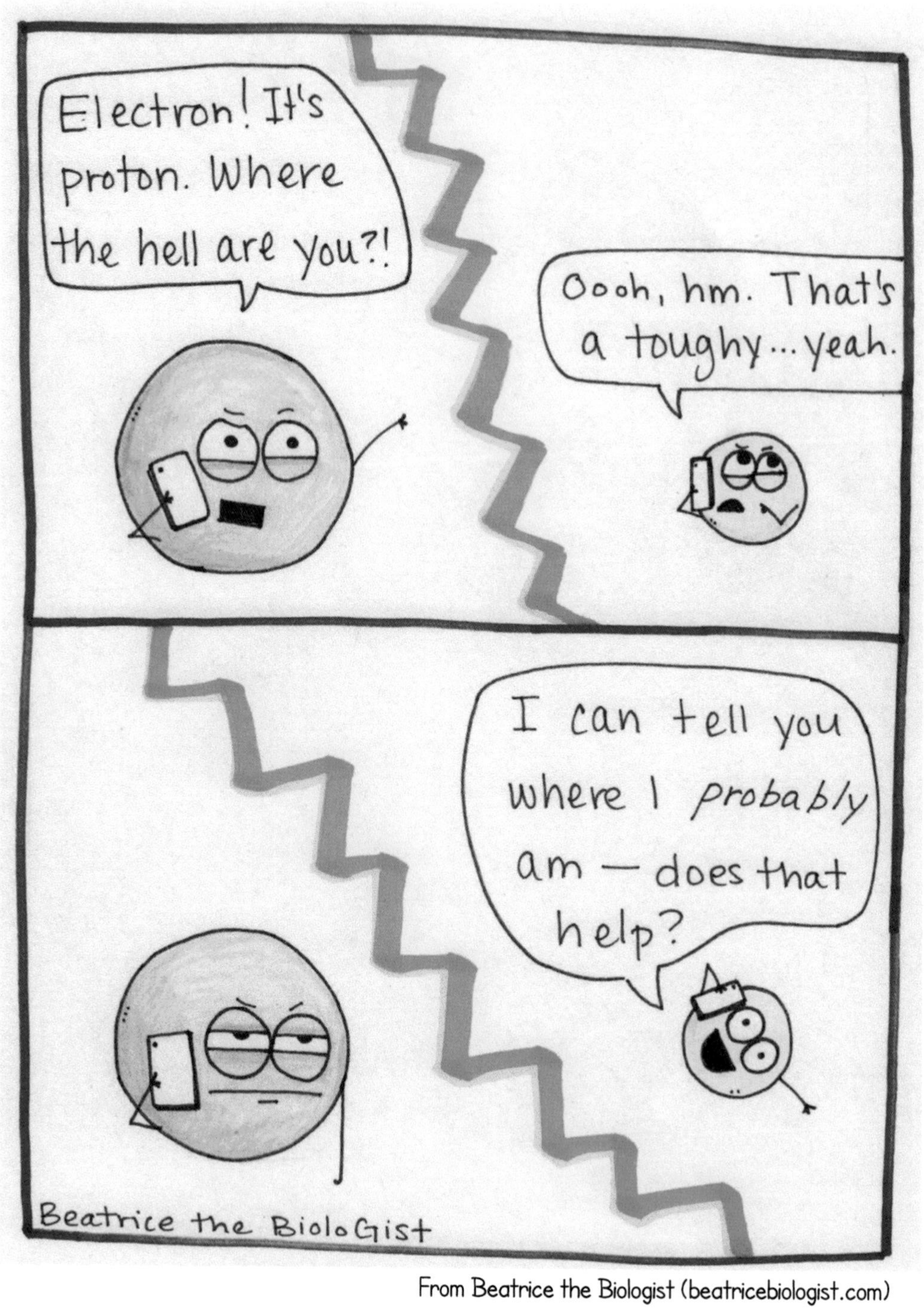
Electron! It's proton. Where the hell are you?!
Oooh, hm. That's a toughy... yeah.
I can tell you where I *probably* am — does that help?
Beatrice the BioloGist

From Beatrice the Biologist (beatricebiologist.com)

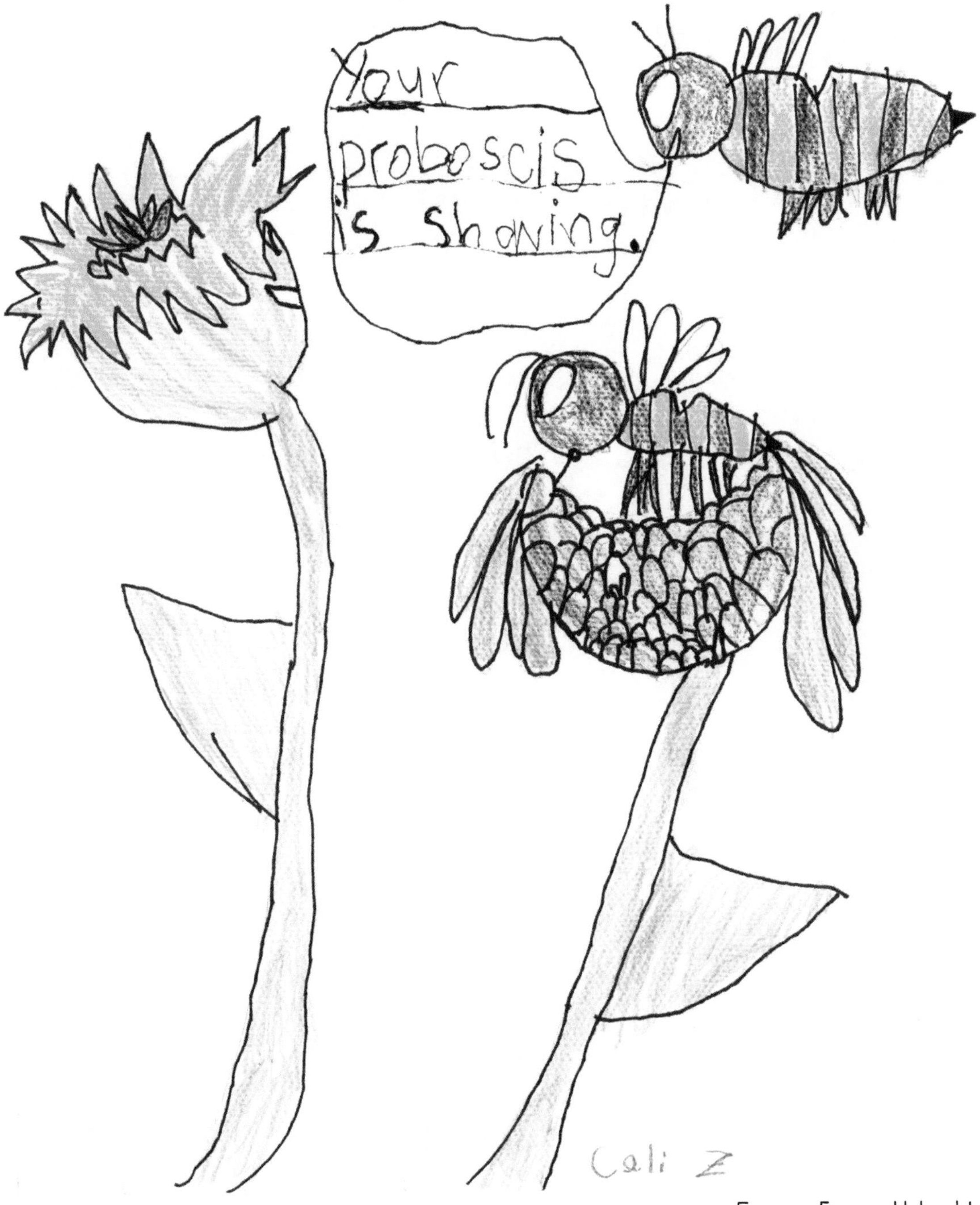
Your proboscis is showing.
Cali Z

From my 5 year old daughter, Cali Zimmerman

View more of my friends' comics through my website, UnearthedComics.com

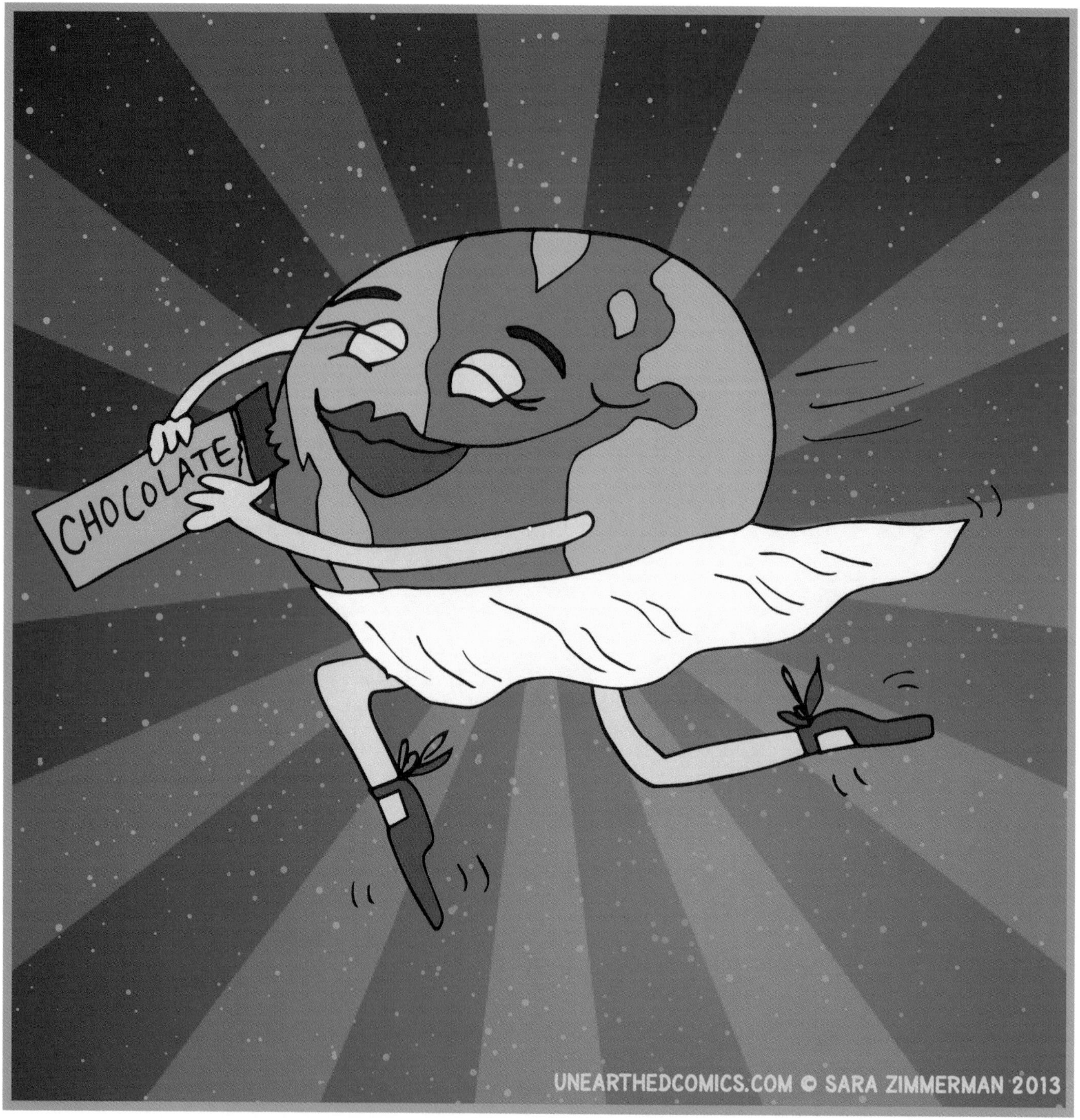
CHOCOLATE
UNEARTHEDCOMICS.COM © SARA ZIMMERMAN 2013

About the Artist:

Sara Zimmerman is an artist who packs each day full by being a mom, wife, business owner, graphic/web designer, illustrator, rock climber, drummer, mountain biker, hiker, snowboarder, surfer, lover of the outdoors, community member, and spiritual enthusiast who loves the colors orange and turquoise and favors the "I can" attitude. Her type-A personality and non-stop tap into the universal creative consciousness has her regularly inspired, touting her famous catch-phrase of being "super stoked" while she enjoys life to its fullest, (except on Mondays when she operates

primarily off of dark chocolate and the promise of a future massage). She gets thrilled when people are enthusiastic about their passion, enjoys most things outdoors, is excited about environmental sciences, and loves living in the California mountains where she can play outside with her daughter and husband year round. SaraZimmerman.net

Check out more comics at UnearthedComics.com and follow on Facebook.

If you like *Unearthed Comics: Unearthing Science*, also check out:

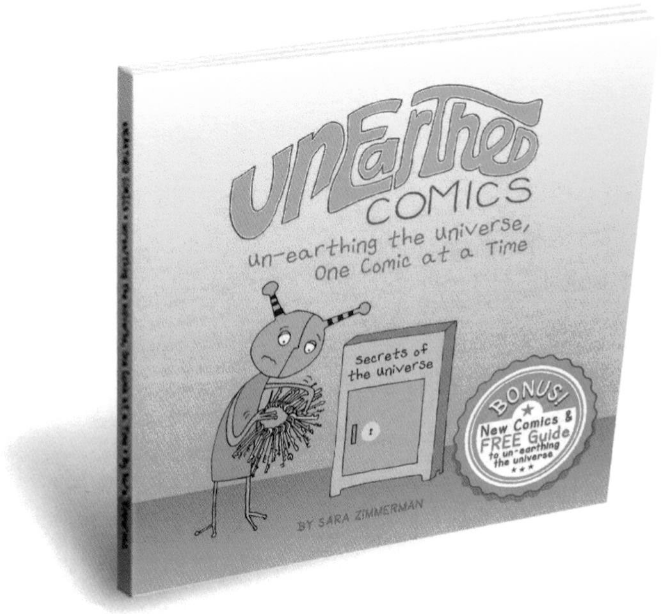

Unearthed
COMICS
Un-earthing the Universe,
One Comic at a Time
Secrets of the Universe
BONUS!
New Comics & FREE Guide to un-earthing the universe
BY SARA ZIMMERMAN

Un-earthing the Universe, One Comic at a Time is the first printed collection of full-color comics from Unearthed Comics' cartoonist, Sara Zimmerman. Unearthed Comics' first popular comics, including "Lemonade Stand" and "Entrepreneur Brain" are presented in this hilarious, full-color collection of more than 60+ business, parenting, marriage, science, yoga, environment, and health comics.

In addition to the book's several never-before-seen comics, *Un-earthing the Universe, One Comic at a Time* includes a special "Illustrated Guide to Un-earthing the Universe": a 5-page, humorous take on new-age teachings and ancient wisdom.

Available on Amazon.com.

24487925R10052

Made in the USA
Charleston, SC
25 November 2013